The Anatomy of a Television Commercial

Thirteen International Awards won by Eastman Kodak's
"YESTERDAYS" Commercial for J. Walter Thompson Company

Diploma
— ACC JAPAN FESTIVAL
All-Japan Radio & TV Commercial Council

100 Best TV Commercials
— ADVERTISING AGE

Finalist
— ANDY AWARDS, Advertising Club of New York

50 Best TV Commercials
— AMERICAN INSTITUTE OF GRAPHIC ARTS

Second Prize
— AMERICAN ADVERTISING FEDERATION

"Clio" Winner
— AMERICAN TELEVISION COMMERCIALS
FESTIVAL

Series Recognition
— AMERICAN TELEVISION COMMERCIALS
FESTIVAL

Silver Phoenix, Best in Television
— ATLANTA INTERNATIONAL FILM FESTIVAL

Grand Prix de Télévision
— CORK INTERNATIONAL FILM FESTIVAL

Finalist
— INTERNATIONAL BROADCASTING AWARDS
Hollywood Radio & Television Society

Special Gold Award
— INTERNATIONAL FILM & TV FESTIVAL
OF NEW YORK

Selected for Exhibit
— LA QUINZAINE DU FILM PRIME
Société Nationale d'Impression et de Publicité

First Prize
— VENICE FILM FESTIVAL

The Anatomy of a Television Commercial

The Story of Eastman Kodak's
"YESTERDAYS"
Winner of Thirteen International Awards

Edited and with an Introduction by

LINCOLN DIAMANT

Past Vice-president Broadcast Advertising Producers Society of America
and Chairman I.R.T.S. TV Commercial Production Workshop

COMMUNICATION ARTS BOOKS

HASTINGS HOUSE, PUBLISHERS · NEW YORK

Published simultaneously in Canada by
Saunders of Toronto, Ltd., Don Mills, Ontario

ISBN: 8038 0348 6
Library of Congress Catalog Card Number: 70-126423

Designed by Al Lichtenberg

Printed in the United States of America

This book is dedicated to all members of the 1969 I.R.T.S. TV Commercial Production Workshop whose interest contributed deeply to the panelists' detailed exposition, and whose involvement is best illustrated by their incisive questions that form the important final part of this presentation.

Contents

Foreword

In the summer of 1968, I was asked by Edward P. Shurick, then president of the International Radio & Television Society, to assume chairmanship of the Society's 1969 Commercial Production Workshop. Traditionally this had been a series of several weekly seminars where, for a modest fee, interested broadcasting and advertising professionals could keep abreast of late developments in television spot production.

To the Society's Executive Director, Robert H. Boulware, I proposed something different for 1969. I began by noting that in slightly more than two decades, the television advertising message — the "commercial" — had become the ubiquitous communication of the United States. TV commercials did not even exist at the end of World War II, yet by 1965 the total number of annual "impressions" they were leaving on the American viewing public had passed the trillion mark.

The time had come, it seemed to me, to commence some sort of definitive analysis of this 20th Century cultural phenomenon (perhaps, even, before it disappeared); one that would enable our own and future generations to better appreciate the contemporary theory and practice of cramming meaningful communication into arbitrarily tiny moments of broadcast time.

Vehicle for such a study, "anatomized" over seven weeks, would be a single significant U.S. TV commercial. I proposed to Bob Boulware that we place this commercial under our seminar microscope from start to finish, rotating professional panels each week to examine each phase of the commercial's complicated development.

The choice of the proper commercial for this study was not as difficult as one might imagine. "Yesterdays," produced for the Eastman Kodak Company by the J. Walter Thompson advertising agency, had been on the air only four times at the time of my conversation with Bob Boulware, but had already gained thirteen international awards for creative excellence. Everyone who ever saw "Yesterdays" appears to remember it quite clearly; it possessed great emotional communication.

It had, in addition, Aristotle's dramatic requirement of *magnitude*, dealing with important subjects and products. And it was two minutes long — an almost vanished breed of costly U.S. commercials. In that length it also encountered a spectrum of creative and production problems hardly to be found in a shorter spot.

"Yesterdays' " creation and distribution were surrounded by great activity. Under the active leadership of perhaps two dozen people, *hundreds* of Americans earning a living from broadcast advertising had invested a total of more than 10,000 hours to bring the sales message of "Yesterdays" to their fellow citizens. The Sistine Chapel Ceiling was finished with less time.

Viewers could merely sense all of this effort. They saw only the commercial itself (one of perhaps twenty thousand produced that year), the finished product — the tip of the iceberg — an implication that suggested to me that the 1969 I.R.T.S. "Yesterdays" seminars might indeed reflect a search *backwards* towards Genesis, or John 1.1: "In the beginning was the word . . ." This eventually became the way the seminars — and this book — were constructed.

The next and most important step was to obtain the cooperation of all the individuals who had labored so long and hard on this unusual television commercial message. Through the good offices of Alfred R. Tennyson of the J. Walter Thompson Co., everyone who had participated in leadership work on the commercial was contacted and invited to appear at one or more of the seminars. It is a comment on the volatile nature of broadcast advertising that several of the individuals who had done creative work on "Yesterdays" had already moved to completely different (presumably more important) positions. But without exception, they all agreed to cooperate by contributing the story of their experiences to the Workshop sessions.

The advertiser, Eastman Kodak, and the commercial production house, MPO Videotronics, were pleased to follow J. Walter Thompson's lead. The pleasant result was a series of information-packed seminars by a group of articulate professionals in January, February and March of 1969 — mirrored faithfully in this volume.

This Workshop offered a unique opportunity to a group of leading advertising film people to step forward and offer a look at themselves and their daily efforts. In so doing, they helped produce this textbook of creative and technical procedures with values far beyond those of mere television commercial production, reaffirming the fact that no one man is a creative island.

It is a pleasure to participate now in bringing this fascinating message to a wider audience.

— LINCOLN DIAMANT

ACKNOWLEDGMENT

The editor wishes to express special appreciation to Eastman Kodak Company, J. Walter Thompson Company, MPO Videotronics, Inc. and their management, creative personnel and suppliers, for all their many levels of cooperation with the Workshop, and in the preparation of this book. Particular mention is due to Robert H. Boulware of the International Radio & Television Society and to Miss Janet Hassinen. And for continuous encouragement above and beyond the call of family duty — to my wife Joan, and to our children: "Thanks!"

Introduction

> "An attic is sexy; a basement is not."
> — *Mademoiselle*, July 1969.

On a Friday morning in April, 1966, Ken Thoren, a senior writer at the J. Walter Thompson advertising agency, slipped a sheet of yellow copy paper into his typewriter. His floating assignment was to continually create "picture-taking" television commercials for Thompson's Eastman Kodak account. Spurred by thoughts about a somewhat fusty Jerome Kern-Otto Harbach ballad composed 33 years earlier for the character "Aunt Minnie" in the Broadway musical *Roberta*, he began to write a two-minute "mini-movie" he called "Yesterdays."

Fifteen months later, on a Sunday evening in July, 1967, television viewers in about six million U.S. homes saw the finished product, advertising Kodak cameras and film.

The events of those fifteen months of difficult creative and mechanical work are summarized in unusual detail in the pages that follow. For the moment, though, we should look a little past "Yesterdays" to the television medium itself.

We live in an economy of accelerated consumption. Every new communications device is rushed into the service of American marketing. With the advent of television, advertisers found an almost perfect living-room selling medium. To quote Erik Barnouw, Professor of Dramatic Arts at Columbia University:

> Constantly changing inclusions and exclusions of frame, attention-riveting magnifications, shifting viewpoints and juxtapositions, interplay and sometimes counterpoint of words, sounds and music — all work to involve the television viewer in a fever of inference and participation.

As a result, in less than two decades, American television advertising has grown into a multi-*billion* dollar business. Today's leading advertiser, the Procter & Gamble Co., spends more than $200 million annually on commercial messages to move its vast spectrum of household products. Compared to P&G and many others, Eastman Kodak is a small TV advertiser; its commercial messages must work artfully and well in the flood of broadcast advertising.

It is a true flood, already attacking the underpinnings of that hallowed American advertising institution, the local newspaper. Advertisers now place a smaller share of their dollar in magazines and newspapers than ever before. A decade ago, newspapers received 31¢ of the advertising dollar —from all sources. Now they're down to 28¢; television (which passed magazines long ago) jumped from 13¢ to 17¢ in ten years.

But the cultural effect of this new medium is more significant. About the time television was being born, Dwight Miner, now Moore Collegiate Professor of History at Columbia, lectured at that University on the importance of national magazines in the cultural life of the American frontier. He spoke of the "national cultural interrelationship" that the traditional illustrated weekly magazines were once able to bring to the isolated farmhouses of America.

He suggested the possibility of an inverse ratio between the circulation growth of the *Saturday Evening Post*, for example, and the decline in the number of farm women committed to mental institutions. Today the *Saturday Evening Post* is dead, while every farmhouse has sprouted a television antenna — a new kind of lightning rod that offers continual protection against boredom. And by being able to *show* rural and urban America what it should be doing (and buying), television is completing the broadcasting revolution *radio* could only begin — and along the way, it has killed off many of our magazines.

The fascination of television — and its advertising — *is* continual. To some it appears merely a new form of insanity. John Cheever has called it "having a continuous automobile accident in the living room." Equally serious critics have asserted it stifles conversation; that it has turned us from a nation of doers into one of observers — and lately, voyeurs.

TV also consumes its own children. "Yesterdays" is interesting in this context: the rise and fall of the full-page magazine advertisement took almost a century; the rise and fall of the *two-minute* television commercial — of which "Yesterdays" is a striking example — may have passed us in in a decade. Already TV *time* charges — which have more than doubled in the brief history of the medium — have struck at the *one*-minute commercial. A two-minute advertising message is a rare holiday dinosaur indeed, and our "one-minute art form" is rapidly being converted into the "half-minute art form."

It all suggests we won't see many more new film (or even video tape) commercials like "Yesterdays" — it seems almost impossible to tell this kind of involved, emotion-charged story in only thirty seconds. "Yesterdays' " length appears to be a necessary function of its undeniably universal appeal — it is hard to visualize any *half-minute* American commercial warranting sustained overseas applause! (see p. 116)

The configurations of the TV medium are also shifting in more important areas than time costs and commercial lengths. CBS, Ampex and others, by introducing the technical breakthrough of the *home* TV playback — television equivalent of the LP record — have now made it physically possible for a viewer to retrieve any TV program at any time. Now that Americans will no longer be limited to watching whatever happens to be on the air at any particular moment, the advertising segment of the TV medium faces its greatest challenge.

Perhaps broadcast advertising people may soon be looking back to the "good old days" — when Ken Thoren could slip a sheet of paper into his typewriter and start 100 or so professionals laboring for fifteen months on a complicated TV commercial like "Yesterdays" and we will all murmur, "How simple it used to be."

1
Printing
&
Distribution

THE PRODUCTION SUPERVISOR

Like an inquisitive jungle explorer cutting his way upstream, this analysis of "Yesterdays" runs backwards — reversing the developing history of the commercial from its last stages to its first. Matthew Harlib was then Creative Supervisor of Television Production on Kodak at J. Walter Thompson Company, in overall charge of the production of "Yesterdays."

Mr. Harlib came to Thompson by way of Lennen & Newell a decade ago, after an extensive background in broadcast writing, direction and production for the three major networks. A New Yorker, he attended Brooklyn College. Since "Yesterdays" was produced, Mr. Harlib has left the agency side of the business to set up his own successful TV and film production group, Adfilm Producers, Inc.

Here he sets the scene for a total analysis of "Yesterdays":

So that we're all talking the same language to start with, let me state what an agency producer is. Then you'll know why a producer (or an agency production supervisor) functions in so many ways, on so many levels, and in so many areas as he does when making a commercial.

If the agency writer is the architect, then the agency producer is the contractor. You can't build a house without plans — the script or storyboard represents the commercial plan. But you also can't build the house unless someone is talking to all the various trades and elements that go

scene 12

scene 10

scene 17

scene 8

into making a house. Someone's got to talk to the plumbers, the electricians, the bricklayers. And that, more or less, is the function of the agency producer. He becomes the pivot around which all the elements of the production revolve.

Now, the function of the producer can be carried on by a lot of different people. There are art director/producers and writer/producers and producer/producers. But the one man at the advertising agency — whatever name he wears — who really gets involved, every step of the way, in guiding and pushing and pulling and kicking and compromising to get the commercial made so that it has a *consistent point of view* — that man is the agency producer.

I'm not trying to narrow the definition; I'm trying to broaden it. Because somewhere in every production, there is one individual who *must* have final say over all the little nitty-gritty things, as well as many of the big things that go into it. That man is the "producer."

Eastman Kodak's "Yesterdays" took fifteen months to produce — fifteen months for a two-minute commercial — from its inception to the form in which viewers finally saw it. Why fifteen months? Because we were *lucky*. This was the type of *corporate* campaign that does not require the viewer to rush out to the store to buy some immediate necessity. And we had the advantage of a client like Eastman Kodak, who allowed us to give this unusual commercial the attention, care and time necessary to bring it to its final impressive state.

It is a totally "manufactured" commercial. By that I mean nothing on the screen happened *accidentally*, unless it was a planned accident. Somewhere early in the production cycle, the decision was made to "manufacture" everything. There are other types of documentary commercials, more or less recorded and filmed as they happen. The stress in those commercials *is* often based on "accidents" — photographing things in a *cinema verité* style.

Not here. This commercial was a completely planned and thoroughly manufactured and produced film. Nothing happened by accident. Patently, a very difficult thing to do. The costuming was as authentic as time and money would permit. (*scene 12*) The old gas station in one of the snapshots was an actual old gas station found in Connecticut. (*scene 10*)

Even the snapshots themselves were artificially aged. Nobody makes deckle-edged prints any more; we found a deckle-edge trimmer to trim the photos to look more like the period they represent. (*scene 17*)

The music was created for the concept. At one point, looking for even more authenticity, I wanted to cut a record and put it on that old Victrola in the spot (*scene 8*), to then play back and *re-record*. But I got talked out of that by our music producer, who promised he could produce the same effect artificially for us, at the stage of production called the "audio mix." It was done very successfully (even the sound of the crack in the record was added artificially, at that stage).

We'll discuss the soundtrack, and all the elements that went into its mixing completion — before it was transferred onto film — including the very important contribution of the music composer and arranger. The mix itself, where all the elements were blended with great artistry and skill, will also be discussed.

We'll even learn a little about the fights that went on, such as what should happen when? At what point the soundtrack should change music-ally from an old acoustic sound to a modern electronic sound — and why, for example.

Nothing in a commercial, if it's properly made, happens just because it happens — but rather because it's *motivated* to happen. Very few things in a properly-made commercial are arbitrary. There are usually good and substantial reasons for something happening when it does.

We'll talk about "editing." Film editing is not like editing *print copy*. Editing film is taking the language of film — all the isolated scenes that constitute the words — and putting them together with visual punctuation marks, so they make paragraphs, thoughts and ideas. As we analyze "Yes-terdays," you'll see how a lot of little pieces of film were combined to make a single strong statement.

This is where the agency producer exercises enormous creative influ-ence — with the writer, with the art director, with the editor, with the direc-tor, and with the *client*, who also has a great deal to say about the end result.

We'll discuss the actual filming of the commercial. The director and agency producer will tell about the location-hunting, and all the arguing that went on: "Shall we shoot this this way?" The writer had originally written this script for a basement, not an attic. I can tell you, there was a lot of blood shed over that move upstairs!

The producer's muscle had more than a little to do with final selec-tion of the attic. But when the writer saw the finished film, he was glad we had twisted his arm. That happens sometimes. Someone comes up with a concept, and may be so involved he develops blinders.

In making a commercial, no one point of view usually holds all the time, except the point of view of *consistent* production which I mentioned earlier. That makes an entity of it. Along the way, there's a lot of give and take, behind-the-scenes conflicts, and compromises.

What it all boils down to, I guess, is that commercial-making was never a one-man operation, any more than advertising is a one-man busi-ness. Members of the creative group, while they act in unison, don't always agree among themselves. But if they act with a consistent point of view, it has a great deal to do with what you finally see in finished form on a TV screen. And the producer is the man who tries to hold them all together.

THE CREATIVE PLANNER

Alan H. Anderson, TV Editorial Group Head at J. Walter Thompson Co., is a creative planning executive who helps organize Eastman Kodak's broadcast advertising schedule, and then provides liaison between client and agency to see everything is properly implemented. Mr. Anderson came to the Thompson Broadcast Department a dozen years ago, after a distinguished first career as a Broadway and summer stock director, and a producer-director during the early years of television. Here he discusses the place of "Yesterdays" in Kodak's 1967 planning, and in their TV schedule for that year:

One of the peculiarities of the Eastman Kodak account is that it's a great account to work on, precisely because we have so little of the classical problems that arise between Agency and Client.

Part of this is due to the nature of Kodak products themselves, and the rest is due to what I consider a deep and trusting relationship between the TV Editorial Group at Thompson and the Broadcast Advertising Director at Kodak. There is daily contact between us, to discuss everything from media to marketing to production — the whole relationship that concerns the TV commercials we produce.

To come down to this one, "Yesterdays"; in our original planning we were sponsoring an NBC program called "The Wonderful World of Color." It had been created by joint effort between Thompson and the Walt Disney people, and the decision to put RCA and Kodak — two Thompson clients — behind the show as sponsors completed a perfect union; both Kodak and RCA at that time wanted to sell *color*; color film and color television. And Disney wanted to sell color films and color cartoons. (Film for color cartoons, obviously, was not as important to Kodak as film for color movies of *people*.)

The TV program was approved, and Kodak began a shared sponsorship that was to last about three and a half years. On July 23, 1967, we scheduled the first appearance on air of the commercial "Yesterdays." It was a "major" sponsorship date for Kodak, meaning Kodak had four minutes of commercial time on that particular date, with two for RCA. The spot was scheduled for "second position" in the show; there was no "first position," since this was a two-minute spot.

At that time, "The Wonderful World of Color" was no longer personally run by Walt Disney. He had died the previous spring, and ratings on the show had fallen off slightly. The program was fed to 203 NBC-TV stations; 99.4% of the U.S. population was theoretically covered. But not everybody turns on their TV sets on July 23rd of any year. They may turn on radios; or go off on vacation.

We later learned the program itself earned a rating of 6,000,000 homes — a 29% share of the audience . . . only 11% of the total available television homes! It was a repeat showing of a WWC program that had been seen the previous winter: "The Horse Without a Head," Chapter I.

It was not an auspicious beginning for "Yesterdays." Fortunately, it was not the only time it was scheduled.

Because I am concerned with Kodak commercials from the moment they're born until the time they're dropped forever (because the product they push is no longer being sold), it's a little hard for me to separate out all the various stages. Let me tell you now about some problems we faced in printing and distribution.

First: "The Wonderful World of Color" meant, obviously, very high-quality color, and Kodak is quite demanding in that area to begin with. They want everyone to see the best possible color in the world. We're extremely conscious of "release print" quality, and are always having arguments about how to best achieve it.

We had 203 stations on the air — fortunately almost all tied into the network feed, without delayed broadcast 16mm film — so we were pleased to know that most of the people in the country were seeing the original top-quality 35mm print, fed from New York *and* Los Angeles.

Second: Since Kodak runs so many commercials, we make up a 25-page schedule on all commercials to be run during the year, showing when they run and what products are involved. There are a lot of Kodak products, and a lot of Kodak commercials; "Yesterdays" was one of three on that particular show.

There are three different selling categories; "Yesterdays" is what we term a "picture-taking" commercial, to motivate viewers to take pictures (and not quite incidentally, to take them on Kodak film). But as you can see, this was stated in only a few words at the very end of the spot. (*scene 42B*) In Kodak's view, people stimulated to take pictures with *any film* (with any camera they happen to have), will probably take them with *Kodak* film, because that's what *most* people have. And then they'll go out and buy *more* Kodak film — we assume.

So we were trying to reach a *family* audience (which is what Disney mostly gave us) with a "picture-taking" commercial. Incidentally, we were also in the process of recommending to our client that we move *away* from

scene 42B

the Disney program, changing our TV media plan to a half-hour show able to produce a broader audience — more *older* family members, not so many children — which would also give us left-over money for sponsorship of other individual programs; what we call a "scatter plan."

And this move did indeed take place, on September·15, 1967, a few months after "Yesterdays" appeared on the Disney show. The commercial was shown once more during 1967, shown twice again in 1968, and shown several times in 1969. Because it was a two-minute commercial, it did not run very often; programming two-minute commercials becomes more difficult every year.

It was one of 87 Kodak spots used in 1967. Only *three* of those 87 were two minutes long.

And of those 87, 25 were "picture-taking" commercials. Another third were "still" commercials, and the final third "home movie" spots.

So we decided the date on which "Yesterdays" would be first aired, and published it in our TV schedule, which goes to all Agency departments involved with Kodak. Thus it went to our Traffic people, who decided from there exactly what had to be done.

THE TRAFFIC MANAGER

Justine M. Somers has been with J. Walter Thompson Company for eleven years, currently as Broadcast Traffic Manager on Eastman Kodak and one other major account. Originally a native of Pittsburgh, she holds·an A. B. in English from the College of Mount St. Vincent.

As external traffic supervisor on Kodak, Miss Somers was responsible for physically supplying the selected media — in this case only the National Broadcasting Company's TV network (and its DB — delayed broadcast — affiliate stations) with film prints of impeccable quality. Here she describes her job responsibilities in regard to "Yesterdays" and the people who helped get her the materials she needed to put the commercial on the air:

Get down to the Traffic Department, and you're in the "non-glamour" side of television production. Even though it's really the tail-end, we like to believe that everything that goes before doesn't make much difference if you don't get the commercial out on the air.

We try to get involved as early as possible in the production cycle. I meet with the Editorial Group frequently, so that we know what they have in mind. I knew, for example, that "Yesterdays" had been in production for quite a while, and that things were proceeding pretty much on schedule.

At a certain point, it became important to assign "Yesterdays" a *number*, for many reasons. The networks will never schedule a commercial by *title*, because they might end up airing any of 49 later revisions of the same spot. The number becomes everyone's permanent reference.

As soon as we got Editorial's schedule, we started drawing up plans for meeting the eventual on-the-air requirements. We knew the air date and the program for "Yesterdays," and it was up to me to contact NBC's Unit Manager for that show, and check film delivery deadlines, location, type and quantity.

People may not realize that every air date is actually preceded by several deadlines. If for example, your commercial is not at NBC two weeks or so prior to airing, you start incurring dollar penalties; if you're *too* late, they may decide not to air it at all, but charge for the time anyway.

So you may be standing there with the world's most beautiful commercial — and you've run out of time! Our job is to see that this doesn't happen.

Each network has slightly different physical requirements for air materials, to enable them to put your commercial on the air to their (and your) satisfaction. For this particular program, NBC required both a 35mm and a 16mm print, sent to its origination points on both coasts.

Their "delay-station" lineup for this show was fortunately very small, but 16mm prints were required substantially in advance of air date, to allow time for editorial assemblage in those show prints.

As soon as I had NBC's information all put together, I got back to Editorial to set a deadline for answer print approval. Their phone usually rings about twenty times a day, with me on the other end of the line, saying, "We're in trouble. You're late."

In this case, however, "Yesterdays" flowed along quite well. We had allowed enough time for it, and didn't have any arguments. (For some "creative" type people, Traffic often gets to be a nuisance; we sit there asking for details to pull everything together, to see that the commercial is aired as scheduled, in the right position, with good quality, etc.)

After I had discussed the air date, I had to leave sufficient time to make my print materials. It's not something done by just snapping fingers; there are no "instant prints." It does take a while to get prints out of the laboratory — and with a client like Kodak, the quality must be as near perfect as we can manage to achieve. That way our commercials will always look good, no matter what kind of color controls the network has set up to handle its different kinds of program material from different sources.

All of this goes into scheduling the answer print approval date. When we did get the approval, I also got the "O.K." to place an order for printing the commercial. I contacted Tape-Films, Inc., and gave them the commercial order — the number of 35mm prints, the number of 16mm prints; not just for the network, but also for all the other "side" requirements of both agency and client.

Our department originates the schedule for both the program and commercial; we advise the networks on all program dates, what spots are to run, what products will be in them — and they, in turn, assume we're going to supply air materials on time.

We have to order with sufficient time for the processing necessary to get out good quality prints. Then if the prints are rejected for any reason, there is still leeway to re-print and meet network deadlines.

We give Tape-Films full delivery instructions. That's pretty much the end of my responsibilities, although after the commercial is finally on the air, I'm still "interfering" with the creative types, because then I also have to *authorize* the talent payments — or "residuals."

We have a group at Thompson that handles the actual payments — but it is up to the Traffic Department to keep the commercial appearance schedule completely up-to-date, by spot number — so we may always know what commercial ran on what date, so that all talent connected with it is properly and promptly paid.

Now we can move to actually getting our prints out, as we sit by and cross our fingers, and hope that after all this work, it actually goes on the air.

THE PRINT SUPERVISOR

Charles Ahto is Vice-president of Tape-Films, Inc., an MPO Videotronics subsidiary handling the "fulfillment" problems of MPO's production operation — which means using completed commercial optical negative material to make and distribute necessary film prints on time to TV stations all over the country.

A native New Jerseyan, Mr. Ahto studied engineering at Lehigh University, and took a job with the Electric Storage Battery Company. His next position was "in film," as Production Manager of DeLuxe Laboratories in New York City. In 1965, he joined Tape-Films as General Manager. Mr. Ahto also serves as a local section manager of the Society of Motion Picture Technicians and Engineers.

His comments here deal with the time-consuming, expensive complexity of the highly-controlled printing stage of "Yesterdays":

Handling this commercial was comparatively easy. With many other clients, you usually have a marketing "pipeline" situation — where product is shipped to break with a particular campaign — and the T.V. advertising film is on a tight timetable. It can be quite a problem.

It would then be ideal to set everything up like this seminar — make the prints *first,* and then go backwards toward the creative beginnings.

Obviously, the greatest single factor affecting the quality of films shown on television is *time.* Here's how we operate, as fast as possible, keeping quality as high as possible:

Negative control point

This is a negative control point. We start here with the optical negative (and a check print) at a specific location. It can be located instantly and sent in for laboratory printing. Our Expediting Department then "chases" this film all the way through our assigned laboratory. We run down the log-jams — timing problems, or actual mechanical difficulties in chemical baths or printing machines. Our client is usually not interested in any of these problems, just so long as we get their prints on the air on time.

The first thing the laboratory does is make out a corresponding print order, and an IBM printing ticket, which also affords raw stock control. When the print is timed and the correct color balance has been achieved, a Bell & Howell strip puncher punches the timing (the amount and character of light) *correction strip* that feeds these printing machines. Remember that many scenes of "Yesterdays" were shot out of sequence, under different lighting conditions — natural *and* artificial — and it had to be "rebalanced" in the laboratory printer to make it look evenly-photographed.

Through a continuous developing machine, the film then flows at speeds up to 250 feet per minute. There can be anywhere from 3,000 to 20,000 feet of film in the machine at any moment. A film break anywhere along the line can ruin all the film in the machine, so you can see why the cry, "Break in the developer" means disaster.

After wet processing, the film passes through a "dry box," then the laboratory is ready to ship the film back to us — the print service.

China Girl

This young lady is called a "China Girl." This piece of film negative, stored under ideal conditions, is used as a color quality standard against which we print all our film. We cut a piece of it into all of our optical negatives sent to a laboratory, and we also give them the numerical settings. This China Girl reproduces ideally at "16-24-20," on a "52-52-52" point scale. If an assigned laboratory cannot reproduce an ideal picture for us at these settings, *they* have an internal problem. This is one quality control check.

High-speed projection

We also go through a high-speed (48 fps*) projection check, and a normal sound (24 fps) projection check, to test samples of printing and film quality.

*frames per second.

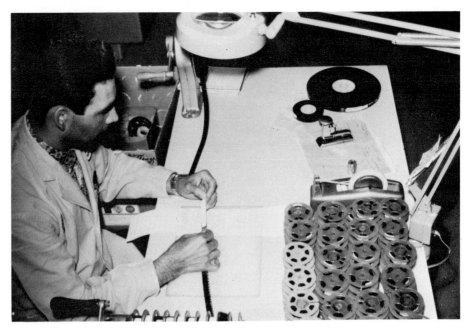

Breaking down single prints

Until now, we have been dealing with the commercial repeatedly printed on huge rolls of film. We cut these apart to put each spot on its own TV station reel.

Print storage

This is our storage vault. Prints are inspected, accepted, broken down, properly identified and placed in inventory, in these bins. Each bin contains approximately 120 prints. Our inventory control records tell us that Spot

#68-0130-120, Kodak's "Yesterdays", is in Bin #136 and there are 22 prints there. Any activity ordered by our Customer Service or Traffic Department passes the Inventory Control Point, and any "ins" or "outs" are immediately posted on the card, giving a current balance at all times. If an agency needs so and so many prints for a media buy, we can check and say at once, "You don't have them," or "We'll have to make them," or "Fine, you're covered." That order is marked with the bin number, so someone can go right there and pull the prints from stock.

Print shipment

And finally prints go out from our shipping department by mail or air express to the TV stations listed in the media buy.

To stay on top of all *our* activity, Thompson has its own color control man who constantly consults with and checks on us, to see that we're doing our job.

THE QUALITY CONTROL SUPERVISOR

Harry "Lou" Leighton is J. Walter Thompson's Color Quality Control Supervisor. A New Yorker, he attended New York University and spent three years in the Navy. He gave up a career in retailing to enter film, working for thirteen years for Film Opticals, Inc. He then went to a succession of other optical houses — K & W, Coastal, MPO/Optico, and Berkey/Pathe.

At Thompson — where Mr. Leighton has now been for two years — he draws on his wide and varied experience with laboratories and production houses to make sure that the best possible film material always gets on the air:

Let us start by considering the "answer print" on "Yesterdays." This is normally the first print to *integrate* the soundtrack and the picture. It is not fully-corrected. At the Agency, I sat with the producer of "Yesterdays" to check the answer print for color quality and to correct any technical defects not apparent in the "one-light"* print that preceded it from the optical house.

Looking at this print, the producer noted any changes or corrections. As indicated earlier, we have 52 degrees of correction in each of three primary colors: yellow, magenta and cyan. This gave us approximately 1,500 shades of correction possible in any given scene. It was the responsibility of the producer who supervised the original photography to determine the ideal color for the film.

This information was then passed back to a laboratory "timer," who put the proper color corrections onto the film. It was sent back into the laboratory for another print. It usually takes two prints to produce a properly *corrected* one. It is this print, in 16mm and 35mm, which must receive the final approval of the producer *and* the client.

Throughout this checking process, it is very important that both laboratory and agency screening room have identically correct projection facilities. Laboratory projection on 35mm uses a Xenon light source, and incandescent projection on 16mm — 14 ± foot candles measured one foot from the screen. To reject a print, it is only fair that the Agency have correct facilities itself.

*An initial mechanical checking print with no exposure adjustments. — *Ed.*

It is most important that the approved answer prints always stay in the can with the printing elements, as a guide to the print procurement people, when they deal with the laboratories. On any large print order, of course, the labs will usually strike a sample print, to judge whether the printing light numbers are holding true on any given scene.

The print procurement people check this sample against the answer print in the can, and give the lab a go-ahead. If the sample print is struck on one machine and the release order is done on another machine, there can be problems. So we try to keep both on the same machine.

Once the lab is printing, Tape-Films checks a random print and so do I, to insure it matches the sample. If it matches — and in Kodak's case it *must* match — only then do we ship. If they don't match, the laboratory must remake the prints.

NOTE: A verbatim transcript of the question period and discussion that followed this and all other seminar sessions begins on Page 125.

2
Soundtrack Completion

THE MUSIC & TALENT NEGOTIATOR

The next stage, working backwards from printing and distributing "Yesterdays," was completion of a single soundtrack perfectly combining all the audio elements — music, vocalist, background voices of the actors, sound effects (such as the auto horn and click of the broken record), announcer, etc. If this discussion lays particular emphasis on the music, it is because more than twice as many words in the commercial are sung than are spoken.

Marion Preston is Supervisor of the Labor Relations Section in the Broadcast Department of J. Walter Thompson Co., and has been active in the broadcast/advertising industry's negotiations with talent since 1959. A native New Yorker, Miss Preston's first and only job — for more than twenty-one years — has been with Thompson.

Part of her departmental responsibility is to negotiate with publishers for the necessary rights to use copyrighted compositions in commercials. It is always important to do this carefully and beforehand (even before mentioning the creative idea to the client), to protect against any misunderstanding or legal complications. Miss Preston's comments indicate the often ticklish nature of her job:

The first thing we had to find out was: How was the song "Yesterdays" going to be used in this commercial? Obviously it was an extremely important part of the action.

Before contacting and negotiating with any publisher, Thompson uses an internal form to find out how a composition will be used. This form gives us the answers to the following questions:

Will the music be used without lyrics? With copyrighted lyrics? With parody lyrics? If the music is used without lyrics, will there be some copy tie-in to the title or lyrics of the song? Will the music come from a recorded work? If so, who is the recording artist and what musical group is on the recording?

Will the commercial be a "wild spot", a local program spot, or used on network television? How often will it be used? Will it be tied-in to any other forms of advertising? Where will the commercial be aired? U.S.? Canada? Worldwide? In what media will the commercial be used? TV? Radio? Motion picture? Other? How long will the commercial be used? How many commercials will use the composition?

In the case of the song "Yesterdays," we learned that it would be used with the copyrighted lyric, a new recording would be made, and it would be utilized in only one Kodak television commercial. This commercial would appear only on network television in the U.S. and be used three times during a six-month period. No tie-in with any other media was contemplated.

Once we knew this information, we contacted the publisher of "Yesterdays", T. B. Harms; we had previously learned that the composer was Jerome Kern, the lyricist Otto Harbach, and that all performance rights were vested in ASCAP.

In view of the very limited proposed use of "Yesterdays", we negotiated a per-network-use fee which was to be paid for each network exposure. Obviously, when a composition is used infrequently, it is more practical and economical to negotiate a per-use fee, rather than a flat license fee for unlimited use. Since the time of our original negotiation with T. B. Harms, however, we have amended our contract to gain an increase in the number of uses and an extension of the time span within which these uses can occur.

The song "Yesterdays" illustrates the caution that must be used in connection with the licensing of copyrighted compositions. For example, the same title may be used for a number of compositions, since *titles* cannot be copyrighted. There are seven listings of "Yesterdays" in the ASCAP catalogue — actually a Beatles composition called "Yesterdays" is probably the most frequently heard. It is obvious that the correct composition, publisher and composer be known before negotiations begin.

Our negotiations for "Yesterdays" are only one example of how we handle the licensing of copyrighted musical compositions. Two other kinds of music are used in our commercials:

Original music may be composed for any commercial — by either a Thompson employee or an outside composer. All original music written for Thompson clients is cleared by one of our musical consultants prior to use. While the advice of this consultant does not guarantee there will be no claims made against a composition, it is a safeguard effort to avoid using anything that may infringe upon copyrighted compositions.

We may use any composition in public domain — *"P.D."* — without prior clearances. Nevertheless, extreme care must be taken to be sure that the *exact version* used is in P.D. There are many compositions that are basically in P.D. but which have actually been revised to some extent; the revised version, in many cases, is copyrighted. For example, the basic composition, "Yellow Rose of Texas" *is* in P.D., but the one Mitch Miller popularized some years ago is *not* in P.D. Mr. Miller wrote some original notes and copyrighted his finished work. Anyone who uses his work without clearance can be subject to a claim of copyright infringement from Mitch Miller's publisher. Another example is "Yellow Bird," the basic tune of which is in P.D., but some years ago Norman Luboff wrote additional bars to the basic composition and copyrighted the entire work. Therefore, if we want to use "Yellow Bird" as re-popularized, it is in copyright and permission must be obtained. Some advertisers and agencies have not been careful enough in checking P.D. music. Their oversights have proved costly.

The use of copyrighted, original and P.D. music can be expensive. Excluding the fee paid for the license of copyrighted composition — or the fee paid to a composer or arranger (if not a Thompson employee) for an original composition or arrangement — there are many other costs involved in using live recorded music. Among these costs are union scale payments to musicians, studio recording costs, etc. If the production budget of a commercial is small and music is required, a producer will usually use "stock music" obtained from music libraries. The customary rate paid is on the basis of the number of "needle drops."* The prices vary but are reasonable.

Regardless of whether the music is copyrighted, original, P.D. or stock, an agreement or assignment letter covering the deal negotiated must be signed by the parties. Thompson has standard assignment letters to cover original music and arrangements. For copyrighted compositions such as "Yesterdays", a contract must be written to cover the terms and conditions negotiated. In our negotiations with composers, Thompson endeavors to obtain all rights, including the copyright, for our clients. The arrangements of P.D. compositions are always owned by our clients. There are usually

*A handy way of estimating actual usage of a recorded composition(s). — *Ed.*

standard contract forms submitted by music library services covering the use of stock music.

Preparing a contract with the copyright owner or publisher of a composition can be a problem. Thompson has certain standard provisions which it uses in contracts, and publishers have theirs. In some cases, there is a difference of opinion as to which form to use. As a result, negotiating the actual contract language can sometimes be as difficult as negotiating the license agreement itself.

Turning to talent, 13 union performers rendered services in connection with "Yesterdays". Eleven were considered "Players" under the jurisdiction of the Screen Actors Guild. Two were "Extras" covered by the Screen Extras Guild.

The 11 "Players" were one off-camera announcer; one off-screen soloist; five on-camera performers; plus four performers whose still photographs were used in such a manner as to classify them as players — and therefore were entitled to residuals.

The SAG Commercials Contract — the 1966 contract was operative in this case — provided for minimum payments for services rendered in the production of "Yesterdays" (and for subsequent uses): these included $90 for the initial work of the off-camera announcer and soloist and $120 per day for each on-camera performer. Payments for air use of a commercial depend upon type of exposure: network, local program, "wild spot" and/or dealer use. In the network category — referred to as "Class A Program" — payment was made for each use of "Yesterdays" on a descending sliding scale over a 13-week period.

The two "extra" players were hand models, under the jurisdiction of the New York Extra Players 1966 Television Commercials Agreement.

Although there are numerous categories of extra players, the two most common are "general extras" and "product extras." Rates for these two categories are different but the payment structure is the same and offers three choices. The one most commonly used is the "buy-out" — which requires a payment of 200% of minimum scale for services rendered. This single payment allows unlimited use of the commercial without any further "extra" fees.

The American Federation of Musicians — under the 1966 Television and Radio Commercial Announcements Agreement — had jurisdiction over the 25 musicians, arranger and copyist involved in "Yesterdays." Their union agreement called for a minimum session payment to all, covering a 13-week unlimited use of the music. Thereafter, residual payments were made for each 13-week cycle in which the commercial was used. These payments, unlike those under SAG and AFTRA agreements, were not calculated by the type of use made of the commercial — network, local program, etc. — but on a flat scale rate covering all uses in the 13-week period.

The only other union having jurisdiction over commercial performers is the American Federation of Television and Radio Artists. AFTRA has several national and numerous local collective bargaining agreements affecting performers in radio and television commercials — live, video tape and film. In 1967 SAG and AFTRA had similar — but not identical — agreements covering employment of performers in video tape and film commercials.

AFTRA and SAG jurisdiction is determined upon *where* a commercial is produced and not *whether* it is produced on film or video tape. For instance, any commercial produced at a studio which is traditionally a SAG signatory is covered by SAG regardless of whether it is produced on film or video tape. MPO is a SAG signatory.

THE PRODUCTION SUPERVISOR

With a green light on music clearance for Kern-Harbach's "Yesterdays" — with lyrics — Thompson could begin creative consideration of the exact way to utilize the piece as part of the complete audio background. Matt Harlib discusses some of the options:

It's not as simple as Marion may have made it sound. When someone hands you a commercial script, they don't hand you a film. They hand you a bunch of problems on a piece of paper. It's a long way from there to a film, as you're beginning to see.

As I said before, "If the writer is the architect, then the producer is the contractor." Part of the production function, as a contractor, is to find people in all the various areas that go into making a commercial with whom you can talk and establish communication. You'd be surprised how, in a business that *sells* communication, the lack of it is the rule rather than the exception. And it's very difficult to find people with whom you can establish more than just superficial rapport. Who know that when you say, "make it black," you don't really mean *jet* black, but you're talking about a dark grey or an almost-black. And it's pretty much the *way* you say "black," or "grey," or "white," that determines the nuances you get in the final product.

I use that specific analogy because the things we are talking about here — soundtrack completion — involve many, many shadings and colorings. Many decisions have to be made in that area alone. For example, "Yesterdays" utilizes every single form of sound a film can possibly use; live sound, voice-over recorded sound, dubbed-in sound effects, as well as live sound effects recorded on the set. It uses echo chambers added in what is called a mix. There are about a dozen different sound elements that had to be coordinated, blended, combined and mixed. And somewhere along the line, at certain critical steps, decisions had to be made as to just how that sound would eventually affect the person for whom it was intended — the viewer. Would it work to sell, and further the ultimate ends of the commercial?

We were lucky — it did; but it didn't happen easily, for a lot of reasons I'll touch on briefly. There were a multitude of directions to go at the mix, in terms of the music, the arranger, composer, and conductor. There were also many directions to go in the choice of the announcer — Bob Landers. It's interesting to note there are only twenty-two words of spoken copy in "Yesterdays" (and for that God bless the client Eastman Kodak, who has a remarkably advanced attitude about what really sells under these circumstances). The decisions, the choices, were made or influenced by Thompson's commercial producer — a man named Warren Aldoretta — who actually did much of the physical work involved in this production.

scene 19

scene 34

scene 31

Before the mix we had this decision to make — what did we want in terms of the musical concept? Did we want the music to "float" all the way through in the old-fashioned manner? Did we want the music to get richer and deeper at the key point where it changes from objective to subjective? (*scene 19*) And did we want the dramatic "break" in the music — from the old-fashioned recorded sound to a modern sound (*scene 34*) — to carry along with the picture when the old record player was no longer playing? All of this involved a lot of discussion.

What we wound up doing, to solve just this one tiny part of the problem in advance, was to record the music two ways. The way it is today; and also, because we had the people there and arranged for it in advance, recorded with no "break," straight through.

Here's where the advertising message came in. As the snapshots evoked the feeling we wanted in our actors, it was in turn evoked in our audience. The music, changing its character, supplemented this dramatic involvement. When we broke the mood and went back to the scratchy record with the car horn, with the record stuck in the groove (*scenes 29, 30, 31*) it was to enable the audience to get ready for the next idea. To give it a moment to catch its emotional breath — its subjective breath if you will — so the next scene wouldn't hit without time to be prepared.

So we recorded two different tracks — the track now used — and a continuous piece of music, which, once it became subjective, rich, no longer scratchy, continued in that vein with a musical bridge into the "Tijuana" brass sound. We got to that sound after a long discussion with Jimmy Fagas, who was the musical composer and conductor picked by Stan Tarner, who represents Thompson's music department. Stan's an excellent musician in his own right, and he participated in the basic concept discussions on how the music should work.

We kicked it back and forth. When Stan suggested the "Tijuana" sound, Jimmy Fagas said, "Gee, I don't know if I can make the transition from this thing to that thing." Stan said, "If you do this, this, and this, you can probably do it." Jimmy said, "Yeah, hey!," and the next thing you knew we were off on a creative bull session, and these two guys were kicking musical terms back and forth that I don't even know the meaning of. But it came out all right, because they were able to communicate and they made a music track that communicated.

THE MUSIC PRODUCER

Stanley Tarner came to J. Walter Thompson Co. — where he holds the title of Music Producer — from Piraeus, Greece, by way of East Pittsburgh, Pa., and a hitch in the U.S. Navy. Along the way, Mr. Tarner attended Julliard and the Brooklyn Conservatory of Music, while drumming, composing and arranging with a number of top jazz groups.

He subsequently worked with the Voice of America and ABC Radio as a producer, served Ted Bates Advertising as a commercial music producer, and moved to Thompson in 1963. At Thompson, it is his responsibility to coordinate all creative composition and the performances required to supply thousands of Thompson commercials with their musical backgrounds. He details how he first became involved with the music for "Yesterdays," and the problems that had to be solved before the musical soundtrack was successfully completed — under his general guidance:

When Warren and Matt handed me the problem of the music track for "Yesterdays," the first print I saw was a rough-cut* George Fineman had just edited.

Since the first half — approximately — of this two-minute commercial had to be fine-cut to a lyric, the first order of business was to supply George with a "scratch" — or guide — track. This was accomplished a few days later in a recording studio, using three musicians and Miss Pat Kirby.

*The initial stage of the edited, spliced picture. — *Ed.*

Prior to that recording, there was some discussion as to whether the singer should be male or female. With the lyric of the song in mind, I was afraid a male singer would sound too pompous (or worse yet, campy) and we'd run the risk of having people laugh, and thus destroy the intent of the commercial. Actually, I thought of Pat Kirby the very first time I saw the picture. Her warm, vibrato-less, almost haunting vocal quality — reminiscent of an earlier big band era — was perfect.

The guide track served a double purpose, since it also provided an audition of Miss Kirby's talent. After hearing it, both Warren and Matt agreed with great enthusiasm that she was the singer for our final recording.

It was obvious that our music for the attic scene with the middle-aged couple would have to be filtered, to get that old "78" record sound. It bothered me that the ludicrous quality of that filtered sound might dominate that entire poignant scene. I wanted to make the music more meaningful as the couple got more involved with their memories — and then it occurred to me (possibly because I'm almost old enough to identify with that couple!) that this feeble-sounding record was, when *they* bought it years ago, as hi-fi as you could get! There was nothing better in those days to compare it with. So at the mix, starting with the needle drop on the record, we began with that very tight, filtered sound.

But just before the first chorus of the song came to an end, we started to reduce the filtering by degrees — almost imperceptibly — so by the time the second chorus started and the couple became completely engrossed in the memories evoked by the pictures, the music is full-blown, and fills the attic with a sound as beautiful as it must have sounded to them when they first heard it. The jarring car horn sounding the arrival of their children is the perfect cue to return to reality — to the old record sound. I believe Matt suggested the stuck record; it was achieved by having the orchestra and singer repeat the first two syllables of the last word of the song over and over again — in 3/4 time. It sounded too metrically precise to me, so I had the audio engineer cut into the vocal of each repeat, giving us the unevenness that we needed.

The family reunion began the second half of the commercial, so our music track then switches from vocal record to film score. At this point, Jimmy Fagas and I had a difference of opinion regarding the nature and attitude of the music underscoring. He felt a modern symphonic arrangement of "Yesterdays" would be very effective. I argued that the song, being in a minor mode and given a serious orchestral treatment, would sound so lugubrious that a viewer would think he was witnessing a funeral instead of a happy family reunion. I held out for the more joyous and contemporary "Tijuana" sound, which was then enjoying great popularity. With Warren and Matt on my side, it was easy to convince Jimmy.

The mixing sessions on this commercial (there were more than one!) were long, but not tedious. Everyone present had his own idea of how it should be done, but I know of no other commercial where the sound track played such an important role; perhaps that's why we were all so critical. After all those weeks of working on "Yesterdays," I was sorry to see it end. I loved every minute of it.

THE COMPOSER/ARRANGER

In 1946, James Fagas — now head of James Fagas, Inc. — was freshly discharged from a U.S. Army ski battalion. He used the G. I. Bill to study guitar and music at the Greenwich House Music School in New York City, was involved with television music, and became assistant to David Broeckman, musical director of the Dave Garroway program, "Wide, Wide World." From there it was just a step into TV commercial music, trying to solve the complicated musical problems of brief advertising messages. Mr. Fagas relates his experience with "Yesterdays":

scene 8

scene 30

scene 34

I remember being called down to Thompson and MPO to discuss the musical problem that existed at that time: When should we start our music? At the very beginning of the film? Or wait? What should we do? After talking, we decided the very best place to start the music was when the needle dropped on the record (*scene 8*). If we started playing before that, the transition of going from a dramatic underscore to the record would not be as effective as if the music started with a reason. And there was a beautiful reason to start playing — the needle had dropped on the record.

Next we talked about the time change, from the past that the actors were reviewing, into today. We wanted to do an arrangement of "Yesterdays" where the needle got stuck (*scene 30*), and we had to simulate a broken record. That created a bit of a problem. Technically, this was our solution: We were in a 4/4 tempo; I switched to 3/4 time and just went "yester-yester-yester-" with the vocalist, to get the effect.

Another problem: Should we play the music track through a filter, to make it sound old-fashioned, or should we play it straight the way it was? We decided to let it go half and half, and later, when the family arrived, (*scene 34*) to really come in with a strong, full blast of music.

The arrangement we wanted was quiet and peaceful, not too busy, and we had to have a good singer. Pat Kirby did a marvelous job.

Then I think we talked about the transition from the record to the dramatic underscore, that changed the feeling of the song. The original thought was to have an oldtime symphonic version of "Yesterdays", with a huge orchestra and strings — I thought with delight that I could make like Maurice Ravel — but Matt Harlib was adamant about going into a contemporary vein. I felt, "Oh, my God! How can you destroy Jerome Kern's beautiful melody, and go into rock 'n roll, or whatever?" At that time, by the way, "Tijuana" trumpets were the big thing.

It seemed difficult to orchestrate and play "Yesterdays" in a contemporary style, still not destroy the song, and yet create the feeling that the family has arrived and it's a great happy "hallelujah" time. The orchestration of the initial background vocal probably took about an hour and a half to write; but it took *three days* to figure out the correct harmonic changes to use going into the contemporary sound!

You won't believe this story. I have a little cat, Matilda. She is very angry with me when I write late at night, and unfortunately I was working late, to get the job done. You've heard of "Kitten on the Keys." About two o'clock in the morning, she's giving me the same business, walking on the keys. This is the exact way it happened; she stepped on a note and, by George, that was it! It gave me the harmonic structure, in the right idiom.

We ended up using a modest string orchestra to back up Pat. There's a slow, one-note transition which builds up, and "boom," we're into "Yesterdays" with "Tijuana" trumpets playing. Pat, instead of singing words, does a vocalese thing with the trumpets. When it was all put together, it was quite good. When I met Matt, maybe a year and a half later, I told him, "You really had the right idea. If I fought against it, I'm glad I lost." I really feel that change makes the whole film. It seems to bring it up out of the ordinary into something different.

I'd like to say one thing about the singers and musicians used in commercials today. There are about 200 top-notch singers and musicians — mainly musicians. The incidence of professionalism here is as high or higher than in any other profession I know. These fellows come in, unpack their instruments, sit down, take a look at their music — and on the first take* they're making the right sounds. All they have to get is a little direction from the conductor, and "bingo," you have a top-notch job.

On this particular commercial, we used 14 strings, 3 brass and 6 rhythm. Some were celebrities. . . . Urbie Green, who leads the orchestra at the Riverboat, is probably one of the world's leading trombonists. We had David Nadian as first violinist; he's also first violinist for the New York Philharmonic. And Joe Wilder, who's a trumpeter with the Count Basie Band. Most commercial musicians are men of this caliber.

*Each attempt at a recorded performance — a "take" — receives a consecutive identifying number. — *Ed.*

That's what I remember about the job. But it's always a ball working with Thompson. Their projects are usually very interesting, and this one was a top-notch project for me. I'm glad to have been associated with it.

THE SOUND MIXER

The next step was to take "Yesterdays'" completed musical soundtrack, announcer track, actors' voice track and sound effects tracks (all "lined up" by the film editor with "start" marks, to play back at exactly the right points) and combine them at a "mixing" studio — Fine Recording, Inc.

Sol Tabachnick, another problem-solver, has been an audio engineer for over two decades. A native New Yorker, he studied sound engineering with RCA and then spent fifteen years recording, editing and mixing at CBS, and also worked for a while in the Film/TV Section of the United Nations.

Here Mr. Tabachnick describes the process of mixing "Yesterdays":

The problems start with what we have "as-recorded" on 1/4″ audio tape; your announcer, singer, music, and effects. First of all, it's in the wrong medium. We work with what is known as "35mm full-coat"; you can record several tracks on a single piece of sprocketed film. This is what we have to go to.

So we go through a generation of transferring, and hope we come out as thrilled as we were with the original. The film editor lined all of this up and prepared it for me. He came in with a cue sheet, which had everything marked down; nothing was done by chance or guess work. The footage was marked and everything done by foot, not by second. He marked exactly where everything came in, where it had to be faded in, where it had to be pre-set, faded out, what types of effects he had; everything completely laid out for me.

So my work really wasn't that difficult, except for the "artistic" end. I had nothing mechanical to do insofar as the film and the track were concerned.

We had three men involved: myself; a projectionist who had the film; and a man in what we call the "dubber room," who lined up all the tracks at the "start" marks. We sat down to discuss it first, and then we started running it. We had to get a nice balance, as an artistic endeavor and also because the commercial sell had to be in the forefront. We can't hide it. We have to enhance it.

CUE SHEET

fine recording INC.
118 WEST 57TH ST.   NEW YORK. N.Y. 10019
212 245-6969
A DIVISION OF *V*idcom electronics INC.

CUE SHEET

SPOT#_____

PAGE#_____ 1

PRODUCER J. WALTER THOMPSON - MPO

PRODUCTION KODAK - "YESTERDAYS"   2 minute version

JOB# 51945   PROD.# 5456   DATE 6/15/67

ANN.	SYNCH VOICES	MUSIC I	MUSIC II	EFY I	EFY II	EFx III	
9 beep				WATCH LEVELS			
				14	14		
	16			in + out			
		35		by		38	
	in + out			Themselves			
	by			40	40		
	Themselves	FILTER				NEEDLE	
						SCRATCH	
		85½ ✕ 55½				85½	
			NO FILTER				
		124½	124½		124½	124½	
	125				BROKEN	NEEDLE	
	LOW	FILTER			RECORD	SCRATCH	
	137	137½	137½		137½	137½	
			NO FILTER				
	166						
	180		189				
			CUT				

AUDIO ELEMENTS
(Actual size)

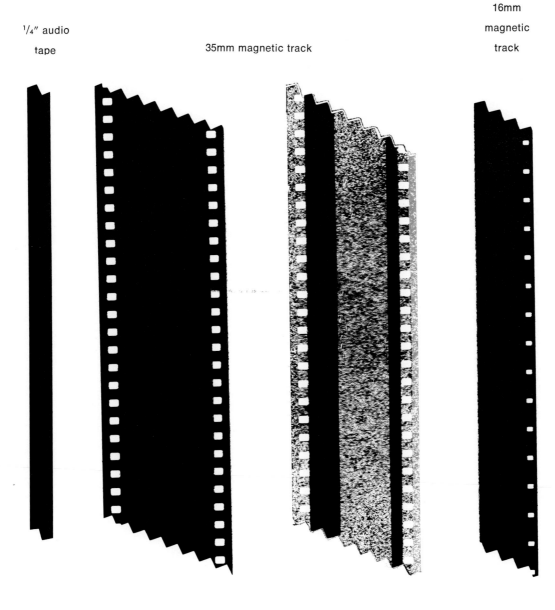

¹/₄″ audio
tape

35mm magnetic track

16mm
magnetic
track

Full coat

"Mag stripe"

Dubbing room

Mixing is a problem, because in a recording session, you usually are working with only one element. If you're recording music, it may sound great. But later, when you play voice against music, something may not hit just right. The same thing happens where an announcer reads a track, and you sit in the recording studio and say, "Gee, that sounds great!" but later.

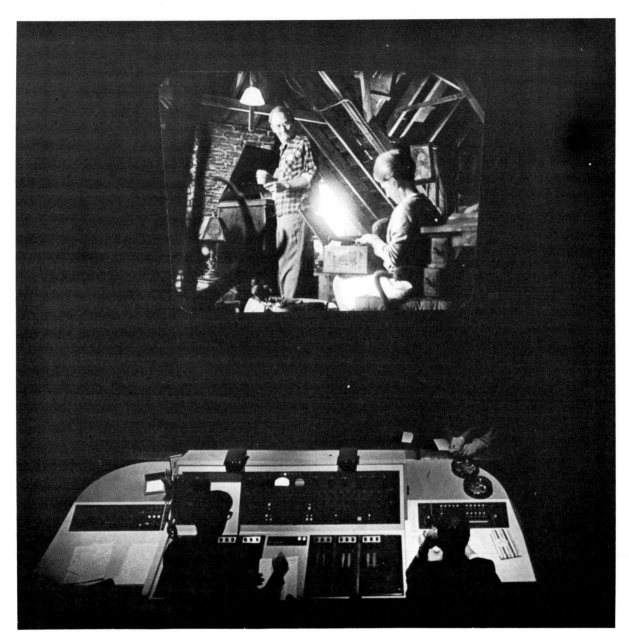

Mixing console

play it against the music track or against an effects track, and there may be something that hits at exactly the same time . . . and you're dead.

Now we go through the process of elimination; bringing the music down, the voice up, or whatever the agreement has to be. The end result took three separate mixes.

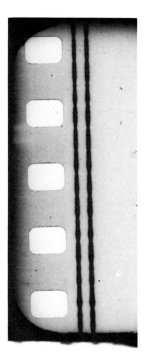

Optical track negative

Optical track positive

Each time we finished a mix, everyone thought it was great. But it went back for client approval and so on, and they found a few things they thought should be corrected or added or subtracted.

I mentioned the dubber man. He takes the various tracks on sprocketed film, and makes sure everything is "in sync" — every "start" mark in the same position. When this is done, they throw a switch — the dubber man and the projectionist — which interlocks the various film dubbers and projector, so that when I push my "start" button on the console, everything runs in synchronization. Unless one of the machines breaks down, it is then physically impossible for something to go out of sync, running either backwards or forwards.

We record on what we call a three-track full-coat recorder, using separated announcer, music and effects. It gives us the later capability of eliminating one track and replacing it directly on the same piece of magnetic stock without changing the rest of the mix.

If the M & E — music and effects — tracks are to everyone's liking, but the announcer for some reason is not, or we have to change copy, we take the master, put it back up, and just re-record the one track. We can actually put in *one note* of music and you'll never hear where, as long as we match levels; it saves the client the cost of going through another complete mixing session.

Whose judgment do we go by? On the first shot, I would say the mixer's. We mix on a large theatre screen with big speakers behind it, to give us the full clarity of the various tracks. Then we take the master mix just recorded and play it back on a closed circuit TV system, an unmodified system, so that the client, producer — whoever happens to be there — can actually see and hear what their finished product will look like. This is also quite representative, because what we hear on the big speakers can be very deceiving; when you get down to that 2″ thing they call a "speaker" on a TV set, the sound is completely different.

Now we usually readjust everything. Again the mixer is given first crack at it. Then everyone jumps on him and says, "No, this goes up and that goes down," and he has to be a sort of pacifist, pointing to the TV set as the truth-box; what is actually going to be seen and heard at home.

From there the master is sent to our transfer room. We transfer it to ¼″ audio tape, put it on 35mm mag film, etc. We also transfer the magnetic element to an optical element; a negative track, which is similar to the negative you get from any photograph. No picture yet, you understand, just sound recording. Then everything is sent on to the optical house.

NOTE: The questions and discussion that followed this presentation appear on p. 130 ff.

3

The Editing Process

THE PRODUCER

Eight thousand feet of 35mm Kodak Film ran through the cameras while shooting "Yesterdays." The commercial was shot about "40 to 1" — 180 feet survived the final editing process that selected and assembled 42 different scenes into the released print. Some "cuts" were short; some were long — the longest is 17 seconds, the shortest less than a second. The man very much in charge of all the creative talents working at this stage of the process was Warren P. Aldoretta, a Producer with J. Walter Thompson Co.

Mr. Aldoretta studied art in high school in New York, and at Pratt Institute and Columbia University. After two years in the Navy, his first advertising job was with Cunningham & Walsh in the "bull-pen"; before long, he was one of that agency's award-winning art directors on four major accounts.

He remained there for eight years, moving to Thompson in 1961, and beginning the slow metamorphosis into a hyphenated art director-television commercial producer that took him onto the Kodak account, under Matt Harlib's supervision:

It has been inferred I know all there is to know about film, and all I can say is that every day I learn more and more about what I *don't* know. It's an enormous area and I'm extremely excited about it. I would encourage any creative person to go into film, along with the warning that his or her life will never be the same again.

Before I discuss the editorial process, I'd like to tell you how "Yesterdays" came into my world as a producer. Actually it all started in the life of Ken Thoren, a writer-producer at Thompson. It would appear that Ken was really at the point where he was ready for something like this to evolve from his own stream of consciousness. Ken's character, his life experience, his love of people; all these ingredients seemed to jell at this time — and Ken came up with a very powerful idea . . . "Yesterdays."

Matt Harlib called me into his office, took Ken's script, and passed it across the table. He said, "I'd like you to read this, and tell me what you think." (*See Appendix B*). He played it very cool. I read the script, and was aware I was reading something special. The only point that really disturbed me was that the concept was designed to take place in the basement of a home, rather than up in the attic. I spoke to Ken about this. Ken's feeling — and this was certainly a valid point — was that the attic had been "done" quite often; he thought the basement would give a more exciting approach. We discussed this at great length. It was not an easy thing to get all of us into that attic, with the greater variey it could offer in architecture and props.

Matt said he thought the concept was as powerful as another commercial also written by Ken on Kodak: "Sunrise-Sunset." He was really saying he felt we had an idea that could go almost as far as that. "Sunrise-Sunset" won numerous awards, including the Grand Prix at the Venice Festival, and was an outstanding commercial. Matt was saying that here was another idea that could possibly — with proper handling — grow into one more powerful selling concept. We were dealing with something that needed nutritive elements brought to it, in all areas.

This was an enormous responsibility, and at the same time very challenging. I was very excited and glad; it was an opportunity to see what I could do to give a powerful idea a life of its own.

I came into film from being an art director; one reason Matt assigned me the commercial was the fact that the motivation build-up of "Yesterdays" depended strongly on looking at snapshots. Stop and look at a black-and-white snapshot; you'll begin to realize how limiting a motivational tool it can be. And we were talking about *old* snapshots, which automatically eliminated color stills for a good part of the commercial build-up.

Secondly, the photographs couldn't look professional. They had to look as if they had been taken by an amateur using a very simple camera. Again we were removed from any professional tricks in building up the motivation; the simplicity was a challenge all around, from the very beginning.

My feeling about editing cannot be stressed too strongly, because I was taught by one of the best professionals in the business, George Fineman. During my early training, George was not only an excellent teacher, but many times he had to spend long hours to make my scenes work cinematically. Otherwise I could have fallen flat on my face. I have mentioned this to George on occasion, but he's a very modest man. He doesn't comment on these things. He was most patient with me in that early period.

An editor is the greatest friend a producer can have. What he brings to film is a marriage between creative intuition and technical mastery, putting emotions and the intellect together into one area.

A good editor must have a working knowledge of directing, be very familiar with cinematography, the use of lenses, lighting and composition. He must have a feeling for music and sound, so he can go to a mixing session and be totally aware of what's really going on. He must understand voice tracks and the subtleties brought to voice. He should be up on fashion, and familiar with animation and all its techniques. Last but not least, he should be a good film editor.

The one guy who really has to have a grip on every single phase of a commercial is the editor. He has to be involved from the very beginning; with scheduling and even with costs. Each time I've worked with George, he has always been two steps ahead of me in practically every phase of our production.

I think you're all aware of the fact that we've gone through a revolution in television. We see writers, art directors and still photographers invading the ranks of film. We have food specialists like Ficalora and Budin, fashion people like Stern and Sokolsky, and many others. All these men have come into film and are making new contributions.

What has happened here? Otto Storch, back in the old *McCall's* days, liberated typography and layout by saying, "We don't have to use just what's popular today . . . we don't have to use a Venus or a Century or a Bodoni. We can use Cooper Black. We can use all the type faces available, provided there's a reason." With this philosophy, *McCall's* pages suddenly went bleed on all sides, typography was liberated and the print art director was on his way.

Today the same liberating forces are at work in film. I'm going to make a statement that may not be too popular with the old school of film makers:

A commercial can most certainly be a miniature film *à la Hollywood*. This certainly is true of a commercial like "Yesterdays," because we're generating our selling story in a very unique way. But remember McLuhan's philosophy, and some of the things he said that tie into this whole area? That the wheel is an extension of the foot; clothes an extension of our skin? So I suggest the television commercial can often be an extension of the printed page.

Many "print" creative talents have come into television and felt liberated, turned on by the fact they could now use music and sound, take still pictures and make them move, take models that usually sit still in a photograph and suddenly allow them to move and tell a story through acting techniques.

More than just making miniature films, then, we're seeing the print world come into the television area; in many cases we're experiencing a simple extension of the printed page. A case in point is a commercial based not on quick cuts or dissolves from scene to scene, but thirty or sixty seconds of just one take. You've seen that with Coke commercials and many others. These techniques are continually evolving and expanding.

We now have multiple TV images — a creative principle long used in print (*McCall's, Look,* and many others) — putting numerous pictures together to assault the eye.

Now — what does a producer like me do on location? How do I get involved in the creative area without becoming a *noodge*?

It isn't easy; in fact it was my greatest challenge. The first axiom Matt taught me when I went out on location was, "Control your environment."

The producer deals with people with enormous egos; who have tremendous talent; who want to do their own thing. I had to cope with emotional actors and actresses, a cameraman who loved cinematography, a director who was really interested in making a feature film in the near future — each of them highly creative and pretty much interested in his own world.

With "Yesterdays," I had to bring all these ingredients together for one specific purpose — to serve my client — so I found myself in one area representing my client, and in another area, trying to work with the creative people and giving them as much free rein as I could, within the framework of what we had to do. This is always my greatest challenge as a producer.

When I go out to shoot, I also have to remember that romantic Bermuda or beautiful Point Lobos soon disappear, and I find myself in a screening room with several people who are only interested in what happens on that screen — especially the client who's paying for it. So what I continually do, any time I'm on location — and this is true for all good producers — is to realize that the name of the game is *what happens up on the screen.* We must control our environment, so that when we get home, what goes on the screen makes sense and does the best possible selling job for the client.

I'd like to say a word about Kodak. I don't believe there's a finer client in the business. The mutual advertising philosophies of Thompson and Kodak have given our creative group many wonderful opportunities to explore really exciting things. They're open to new ideas, they're willing to listen to new approaches, and they give us green lights whenever they can.

scene 9

scene 2

scene 18

scene 13

Without that freedom, many of our accomplishments could never have happened.

Now, as far as "Yesterdays" is concerned, our primary concern was the fact that the situation in the attic was very static. The actors were sitting close together, looking at static black-and-white still pictures. (*scene 9*) What could we do to make it emotionally involving and hold people's interest?

First, we had to tell the viewers where we were situated; a master opening scene of a picturesque attic filled with fascinating objects and family history. (*scene 2*)

Note how the director planned this scene that allows the actors to discover the pictures in the old box. This could have been a very corny piece of business; it came off believably because Mike thought it out well.

Notice that when they pass pictures from hand to hand, it is designed in such a way that when she looks at a photograph, she passes it on to him and vice versa. (*scene 18*) This was studied very carefully, and shot separately from the rest of the commercial.

Another thing to note is how Mike created the feeling that these two people loved each other; an actor and actress who may not have even seen each other before.* How does a man direct this — two people who love each other, sitting in a very static situation, looking at snapshots? Many little nuances do a great job. (*scene 13*)

Study how the people showed they were being deeply moved by what they were seeing. Little subtle things again, with hands and gestures. And finally notice the lighting, and the shots made by the cameraman at many different angles, to create a deeply moving, different kind of experience for every viewer.

THE EDITOR

George Fineman, employed as a Senior Editor at MPO Videotronics, Inc., was assigned to edit Eastman Kodak commercials exclusively, under a special arrangement with J. Walter Thompson Company. Mr. Fineman has been busy in film for forty-five years, beginning his career with Consolidated Film Industries in silent film title production. With the advent of sound, he moved to Paramount in charge of special effects, and produced the famous "Eyes & Ears of the World" end-shot for Paramount Newsreel.

Since 1954, Mr. Fineman has handled TV commercial completion chores for Eastman Kodak at a number of important pro-

*But they had. See Evelyn Pierce, p. 85.— *Ed.*

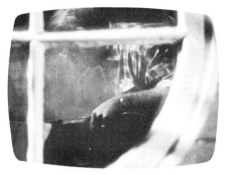

scene *1A*

scene *9*

scene *11*

scene *23*

duction houses, including Filmways, MPO and Howal Film. Here he describes the particular problems of selecting and piecing together the various scenes Mike Cimino shot for "Yesterdays":

If you get good footage, you can do good things with it. Even so, part of the intended concept and story line went by the boards.

It was Mike Cimino's intent to keep the story constantly on the camera move, so we faded up to the exterior of the house and saw Grandpa through the window drop the old trunk. (*scene 1A*) We moved inside as we went past him, saw Grandma coming up the steps with a pitcher of iced tea. We constantly kept on a camera move until they both got to their final positions, looking at the pictures. (*scene 9*) It was planned as a continuous move.

This had to be dropped, because of the time we needed to play up the old snaps and the reactions to them; and the time needed at the end of the spot for the "sell." This made it necessary for us to entirely eliminate the iced tea sequence, and Grandpa with the can of soda he drank. It made us get into establishing the phonograph, the song, and the real gist of the story as quickly as possible.

I must say, however, that through the efforts of the people involved in planning the shooting, we found ourselves with an abundance of working material. Approximately 8,000 feet of dailies was certainly ample coverage to make this work either way.

After filming, we had all the takes selected for possible use weeded out from the full shooting, and printed up as what we call "dailies." As we screened them, we studied them, looking for all the possibilities each take had for a particular use.

A take used may have had a certain bit of action we liked, or the timing may have been better, or the match-cut to an incoming or outgoing scene might have worked better. Much overlap action was shot in any one take, to give the editor freedom at the Moviola.

Little touches that work in the editing give that little extra something often not thought of at script or storyboard time. They gave the picture an added dimension, tempo and mood.

Look for the touch where Grandpa reacts to the college snapshot of himself — with a full head of hair. (*scene 11*) Today, his hairline has receded. Or look for other touches such as the light bouncing off the edge of the eyeglasses, or the eyeglasses match-cut, from snapshot to putting them on again, to give a little more pace. (*scene 23*)

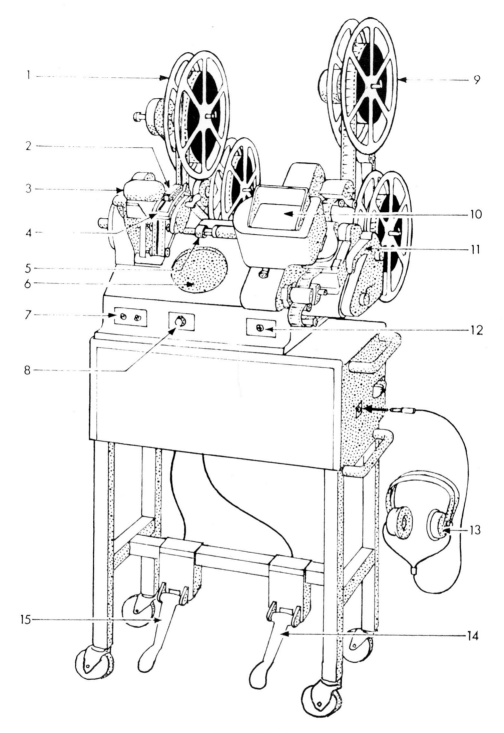

MOVIOLA

1. Sound track take-up reel
2. Magnetic track sound head
3. Optical track sound head
4. Sound gate
5. Sound/picture clutch
6, Speaker
7. Sound-speed motor switches
8. Speaker volume control

9. Picture take-up reel
10. Picture screen
11. Sound/picture brake
12. Variable speed motor switch
13. Accessory earphones
14. Foot control for 12
15. Foot control for 7

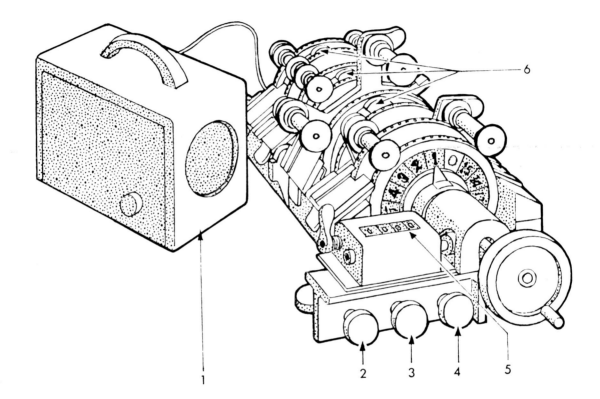

SYNCHRONIZER

1. Reading amplifier/speaker
2. Three-track volume controls
3. Three-track volume controls
4. Three-track volume controls
5. Footage counter
6. Magnetic track sound heads (under film)

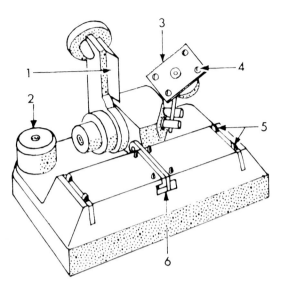

SPLICER

1. Cutter blade
2. Splicing tape holder
3. Serrated-edge tape depresser/cutter
4. Clearance holes for registered pins
5. Registering pins (end)
6. Spring-loaded guide bar

(Illustrations modified from *The Technique of the Film Cutting Room* by Ernest Walter, © 1969 Focal Press Ltd.)

scene 1

scene 42B

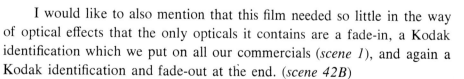

I would like to also mention that this film needed so little in the way of optical effects that the only opticals it contains are a fade-in, a Kodak identification which we put on all our commercials (*scene 1*), and again a Kodak identification and fade-out at the end. (*scene 42B*)

Looking at the "outtakes" — the material we did not use — I think it's only fair to say there's a full five minutes of other angles not in the rough cut. It probably would have made a great featurette, better perhaps than some shows now on the air.

THE OPTICAL TECHNICIAN

The few optical effects required in the "Yesterdays" negative were supplied at the "optical house," Cineffects, Inc. Robert D. Pittluck, now executive vice-president of Cineffects (and their subsidiary color laboratory) started with the firm more than two decades ago as a "can carrier", almost before there were TV commercials. A New Yorker, he attended Hofstra University.

Here Mr. Pittluck shows the way Cineffects handled the work Mr. Fineman began:

Let me run through the steps we go through to get from George's edited workprint to the finished print. First, we make an interpositive, a product with a yellow dye background. It doesn't look much like the print, but it has all the information necessary to reproduce a duplicate of the original negative.

Now, back to the negative, but not the original negative shot in the camera. This dupe negative — or "internegative" — is made for many reasons; one of which is to add the optical effects, of which, as George pointed out, there were not too many in this spot.

The end result is a print off that optical negative, with the addition of a soundtrack as a release print.

In "Yesterdays" as in almost all film commercials on the air, the entire spot was reproduced from an optical negative. There are many reasons; I'll go into a few. Due to the number of cuts that are made and the amount of handling, it would be unwise to physically expose the original negative to the steps it would have to go through in getting to final air prints. The first thing done after the workprint is struck and scenes selected to be used in the final spot — these scenes are pulled and a protective "interpositive" made of all of them.

In making an interpositive, a great deal of control has to be exercised Before the interpositive is struck, the negative is taken and timed very much the same way the final optical negative is timed for printing. Our technique is to take that negative and put it on a color video analyzer, and run it through scene by scene, correcting the exposure to as nearly the way the editor has told us he wants it.

For example, there may be scenes he deliberately wants timed lighter or darker from the way they appear in his work print. There is often quite a bit of color variation from scene to scene in the dailies, shot at different times and printed at different times.

Color video analyzer

PRINTING FLOW DIAGRAM

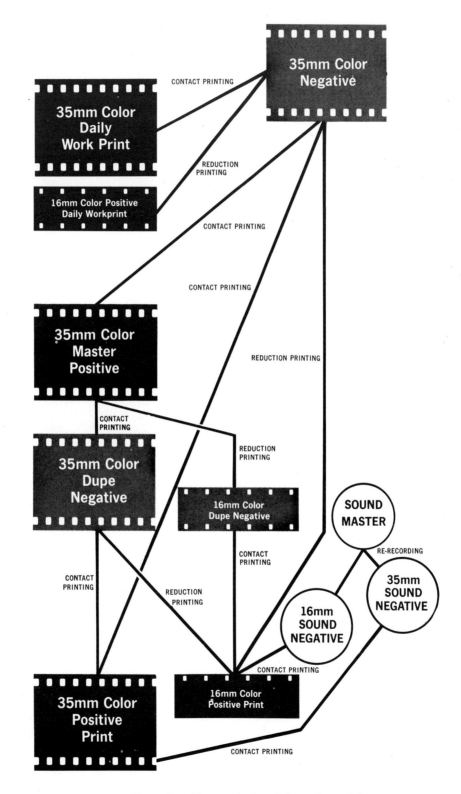

Reproduced by permission, DeLuxe General, Inc.

Part of the reason for going through an optical negative is to even out the exposure, and provide a negative which will print well in the lab. After the negative is timed, and the interpositive material struck and developed, that interpositive then goes through a procedure similar to editing. It's a matter of picking out the portions of the scene that match the work print, putting them in proper continuity and preparing a log sheet — which the optical cameraman then interprets to rephotograph from the interpositive to a new negative. This negative goes into the lab.

Before this negative can be struck, however, it's again necessary to take the interpositive and run a series of Cinex tests on it to pick the exposure for each scene, so theoretically when the optical negative is finished, it will print on a single "light."

I say "theoretically," because it never quite works out on one light. Every timer has his own idea of what he'd like to see in the final result. So we just try to make it as consistent a negative as possible.

This layout man, with a work print up, is preparing the interpositive and making out his work sheet, to direct the optical cameraman in rephotographing the scene.

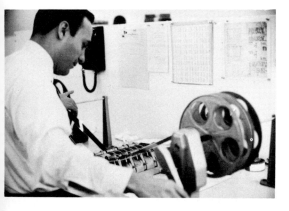

Laying out the job

This represents another stage — on the timing board is a series of Cinexes. There is a range of color in each one of those steps, plus a range of density. The timer, matching one to the other, evens up the exposure or creates the degree of exposure indicated on the sheets that go to the optical cameraman.

Another behind-the-scenes but very important step is cleaning all the film used in each step. It has to be spotlessly clean, if the negative goes through three or four steps before the final print. Any dirt added in each step is multiplied if it's not cleaned off at once, so we use a sonic cleaner to remove accumulated dirt.

Checking Cinexes

Sonic film cleaning

Optical printer

This is part of our optical camera room. The interpositive is run in one of the two heads on the left hand side of the printer, and rephotographed in the camera on the extreme right, adding whatever optical effects are necessary.

Here you can see these complex machines in closeup.

Close-up,
optical printer

Operations room

Here's an overall shot of our operations room.

Most spots use more optical effects than "Yesterdays." There is no criterion for the amount of effects. Some very good commercials, even features — I'm thinking of "High Noon" — have been made without a single optical effect; just straight cuts — very much the case with "Yesterdays."

A lot of commercials rely quite heavily on optical effects. Part of the difficulty in editing is that the editor has to visualize where to use his effects. We put them in, but editors first have to visualize them with cuts, with just the marks (see *Workprint Markings* on following page) to indicate effects. and without the effects themselves. Effects are not just transitions but a very real pattern; our job is to get the editor's workprint onto the screen in the form of a finished, integrated piece of film, carrying all his creative ideas.

This whole process is a series of links. If at any stage it breaks down, it destroys what went before, and whatever could go on after it. If the optical dupe quality doesn't hold the quality of the original, the original might just as well not have been shot properly in the first place.

NOTE: The questions and discussion that followed this presentation appear on p. 135 ff.

STANDARD WORKPRINT MARKINGS
TO INDICATE EFFECTS

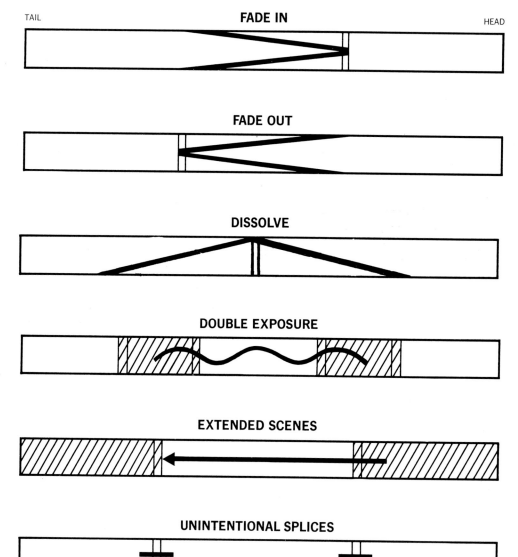

FADE IN

TAIL

HEAD

FADE OUT

DISSOLVE

DOUBLE EXPOSURE

EXTENDED SCENES

UNINTENTIONAL SPLICES

Reproduced by permission, DeLuxe General, Inc.

4
Filming
The
Commercial

THE PRODUCER

As you have seen, the gestation period of "Yesterdays" was lengthy. But a commercial is not only months of ideas or discussion or re-evaluation — eventually talk-time is over, and it must become a piece of film. Camera magazines must be loaded, switches turned on — and the "moment of truth" is at hand.

Before that moment much planning takes place, but this chapter deals primarily with the "moment of truth" itself, when filmic execution begins. Like many Kodak commercials, "Yesterdays" possessed an additional photographic complication — it consisted of motion picture photography of previously-photographed still photographs.

Obviously a problem in logistics, further complicated by the fact that the still photographs in "Yesterdays", showing a married couple at various stages of their life, all had to be "made to order". The way that particular problem was handled adds special interest to this filming discussion, begun by Warren Aldoretta:

As we approached our shooting date and the choice of a production house to do "Yesterdays," there was a great deal of thought and evaluation given to that decision, It was not just something that "happened." There were many people involved, and we talked to many companies.

One man, the director Mike Cimino, was very much a part of the original enthusiasm and feeling for the "Yesterdays" idea. Let me tell a story about myself. Once the script was given to me, I had strong positive feelings about working with Mike Cimino. I had seen his "reel" and was very impressed with it. He brought to his commercials excitement, taste, energy and tremendous awareness. But one thing did concern me about using Mike for "Yesterdays." We were dealing with a story about people in their fifties; Mike is only in his late twenties! I was concerned, because as successful a director as Mike had been, did he really have all the living experience necessary to be able to feel and direct the subtle nuances necessary to make the story come off, and build its emotion?

I talked frankly about this to William Susman of MPO. Bill spluttered a few words, a bit more in shock than anything else. Because at this point Bill knew more about Mike's talent than I did. He had absolutely no doubt that Mike would be completely capable of bringing to the film all the style and sensitivity it required.

I have always been grateful to Bill for that advice, because obviously he knew his man.

THE FILM HOUSE PRODUCER

William Susman is Executive Vice-president of MPO Videotronics Inc. (the initials stand for the last names of the company's three founders), one of the world's largest television commercial production firms. Mr. Susman came to MPO fifteen years ago after becoming discontented with a career in industrial engineering. He began at the bottom of the new ladder as a "gopher" (go-for), moved up to "AD" (assistant director), then became studio manager and a corporate executive.

On a job of "Yesterdays'" importance, it was Mr. Susman's personal responsibility as the MPO house producer to weigh all the potential cost factors involved and estimate a competitive production price for Thompson's (and eventually Kodak's) approval:

A producer in a TV film production company is not just the film company's producer; he's also its salesman. The problems he faces when dealing with someone from an advertising agency are many. First, an analysis of the person he's dealing with. In this particular case, I was dealing with a man who had just become a commercial producer. A man who had been an art director, who was very sensitive, artistically talented, and who would therefore analyze proposals from an artistic viewpoint. As a good salesman, I had to leap forward with the best artistic talent we had available.

Secondly, you look at the man with whom you are dealing and estimate his influence on the cost of the job. Not just in terms of your knowledge or your experience or your hope about how long it should take to produce. You not only estimate the job, you estimate the man. You know full well that with one man, your shooting will be two days, will be accomplished in sixteen hours and will use 4,000 or 5,000 feet of film. You also know that the very same commercial with another man may well run three days with five hours' overtime and 7,000 feet of film.

You not only cost-estimate the agency producer; you must also take into account the way your *own* director works. Let's face it, once the director takes off on a project, it's *his* baby. If he really is a good director, (as Mike is), no one is going to tell him at some point, "Mike, don't do this, or that."

Mike may say, "Okay," but he'll still do what he wants, because he has his own way of achieving the objectives he is after. As with any talented artist, he cannot be told how to paint, or how to write, or how to picture, or how to visualize. Therefore, the film company producer not only analyzes the man he's dealing with as buyer, but analyzes his own company's talent and comes to a conclusion about how to price it.

There are many other things that go into this mix. If you're introducing new talent, of course, you may go in with a little bit lower price.

The next thing the producer must do is decide whom he is going to try to assign to this job. In the case of MPO, we have a tremendous staff in terms of number of directors, cameramen, grips, props, electricians, etc. We have over 384 permanent employees, aside from people we put on when we have increased business. So it is possible to assign various kinds of talent to various kinds of jobs.

You analyze whom you have available; who would be right for the project. And then, frankly, you try to sell the best man available. For this job, it was obvious that Mike's visualization and Gerry Hirschfeld's photography were a perfect combination. Of course, MPO can take only partial credit for the beauty of this particular commercial, because a good commercial begins with the idea, and the idea begins with the agency. But MPO produces between 10%-11% of all the commercials produced in the United States, and if you'll look at our record of prize winners, you will find that we have 10%-11% of the prize winners, year after year. So we must be doing something right.

When you do get a good commercial idea, it's important to use good talent, so the best within it may be realized. We had an extremely fortunate situation. We had a sensitive producer (Warren), who was willing to go

scene 2

along with our recommendations. We had a superb director, a great camera-man, and a wonderful designer, Karl Hueglin, assigned to the job of building the set.

The set was built on one of our smaller stages. When I had to analyze and estimate the cost of "Yesterdays," of course I estimated the cost of building that set. You try to figure out the camera angles; you talk to your director and find out how he intends to shoot. (*scene 2*)

In any case, the time you estimate for the job depends on your experience with the director, the number of set-ups he has*, and the cost of the set (dependent of course on the camera angles).

Another fortunate thing occurred here. Sometimes costs themselves determine a course of action, and perhaps a fortuitous course! When Matt Harlib first came to me, he wanted an estimate only on our shooting the live action. He considered using some outstanding still cameramen to do the still part. I was strongly against it and heartily underwrote the ability of Mike and Gerry to do both. Then it turned out that the money involved made it prohibitive for Thompson to use any famous still source. The talent — that did *all* the photography — was a superb choice; a case where initial money problems led to a very happy conclusion.

THE DIRECTOR

Brooklyn-born Michael Cimino received his B.A. in Fine Arts from Michigan State University, took additional courses at the Illinois Institute of Technology, and then moved to the Yale Graduate School of Design for his M.A. in Architecture. He entered film as an editorial assistant, and worked his way up the creative ladder to a point where — after four years at MPO Videotronics, Inc. — he was one of the most sought-after young commercial directors.

His work on "Yesterdays" added to this acclaim, and stoked his ambition to move into feature film work. He is currently in Hollywood, working on his first feature. Can Mr. Cimino bring to this new area the same degree of tireless concentration and detailed effort that he perfected in the television commercial field? For someone who has also been an architect, book designer, fine artist and still photographer — it should not be too hard. Here, Mike Cimino waxes both concrete and philosophical on the shaping of "Yesterdays":

*There were over fifty set-ups (used and unused) required to film "Yesterdays" — plus the preliminary still set-ups. — *Ed.*

Any film really is the result of so many people's contributions from so many areas, that it's difficult to know where to begin. I think the best I can do is describe the basic methodology — the basic approach we had to the work.

We were able to make a very fortunate choice of talent — Sarah Meade and Kipp Currie. Most of the effectiveness of the commercial really stems from the work they did. The most sensitive moments in the commercial are really something I had very little to do with. It's something that came directly from their own personal work.

To begin with: The Casting Session. I would say the primary purpose of any casting session is *not* to have people read the material prepared for them; *not* to hear them say the lines prepared on a script or storyboard.

The most valuable thing you can do in any casting session is to see how *flexible* people are. Devise some way to let them reveal aspects of themselves you might not normally see. Reading lines prepared for them in script or storyboard presents for most actors very limited range to say or do anything.

In this particular case, we did something on the spur of the moment; I'm sure Sarah and Kipp remember it. We had them dance. They were simply dancing around the studio, and we played music and had them read their "composites*" to each other. As they danced around, she would say, "I had two years at the Arena Stage," and he said, "I studied at the American Academy of Dramatic Arts," or what have you.

An unorthodox way to approach casting, but a lot of things came out — a lot of little things that normally you would not have seen had they just read some lines, or if you looked at their profile, or the back of their heads, or whatever. It's important to look for something you might use. It worked out very well. We had people coming in pairs; Sarah and Kipp happened to come in together, and it happened they were perfect, and we used them.**

Basically, you must make casting decisions on an intuitive basis. You really have to go with the feeling in your stomach, as opposed to your head. There are no definite rules that you can formulate to pick someone, and it can't be done by a committee — by five or six people — because inevitably you get a general feeling with everyone trying to make some well-meaning contribution. It does not work. It must come from one person.

On every job, that person must be the director. There are no two ways about that. It must come from him. I — and everybody else — have done commercials where that decision has been altered by circumstances, and we

*A representative selection of the talent's professional photographs, printed on a single sheet with acting/commercial credits on the reverse side. — *Ed.*

**But Evelyn Pierce's casting calendar (p. 85) suggests the actual decision was a bit more involved. — *Ed.*

had to make adjustments. But the effect can never be as strong as when the director himself feels some intuitive connection with the people he thinks are right. It's to Warren's credit — particularly since he was a first-time producer, that he allowed me that freedom. It paid off. I think it would pay off more often if other producers did likewise. It has nothing to do with ego, or one's position as a director; it has only to do with the end result.

I think on a film — particularly one like this — there has to be (to use an overworked phrase) a great deal of love among the people making it and the people in it, in order to get results. Those results don't come from calculation. They come from everyone having genuine enthusiasm, always a most difficult thing to get.

With all the solemn pronouncements of how wonderful the commercial is, etc., I don't really place much stock in those thirteen awards. I don't think that ultimately they mean very much. I think the fact that people generally accept "Yesterdays'" is very nice. I enjoyed it a great deal.

Curiously enough, the thing that I looked forward to doing in it the most was doing the stills. After the initial casting was completed, we faced the problem of shooting the still pictures. My memory of the job is that it was a great deal of fun; it was something quite different.

We approached the stills the way we would approach any film job — we went out and scouted locations, after researching the different periods we wanted to capture in each individual picture: 1934, 1935, 1938, 1940, 1942, 1945, 1953, and 1961.

Our initial group consisted of make-up artist Andy Ciannella of MPO, hair-stylist Betty DeStefano, wardrobe people from Thompson, Warren, our art director Karl Hueglin, and myself, all working together to choose items for each period. I usually try to involve an art director in every phase of the work, whether it has to do with selection of hair or make-up or whatever. I think it important he be there. I have used art directors on location jobs where normally you would not use one — to make suggestions, to come up with new ideas, to modify old ones.

In this case, all the people who would ultimately create the commercial were working together right from the start. People weren't brought in at various stages. The art director was with us when we selected wardrobe. The hair-stylist was with us — as was the makeup man — when we discussed the set. Everyone could feel the thread of the thing all the way through.

The next step, using old magazines, photographs and films, was to decide what make-up and hair styles we would like to use for each period — and what wardrobe. After we found, through scrap material, the hair styles and makeup we wanted, we made a large chart of the different years — indicating what style would be used in each, what color, what hairpiece, if any, would have to be created. We even attached pictures to the chart, so that when we finally arrived on location for the stills, the make-up and hair people not only knew what style to go to, they had a picture to eliminate any confusion.

As with all film productions, we made some modifications when we looked at things three-dimensionally. Basically, however, all decisions regarding wardrobe and hair were made in advance.

We spent three or four nights up at Eaves Costume Co., picking out wardrobe and trying it on Sarah and Kipp. Everyone participated in expressing opinions about the style of a period; eventually we arrived at a look for each still — wardrobe, hair style and make-up.

In Kipp's case, it was complicated by the fact that we had to continuously change his hairline. We changed his hairline all the way through the still filming. We padded him out in some sections. But with our master chart of what he should look like, there was no confusion.

The next phase of the work was to go out and select period locations. This was done the way normal location scouting is done, by the assistant director and me. Most of the locations in the stills were shot around Danbury, Connecticut. Most of the buildings are fairly authentic as to period and year.

scene 12

My general working method is not to lay out any shooting, be it stills or motion picture, until I have made photos of the entire location. If I have time, I make shots of the location at various times of day to see what the light is doing so that shooting can be planned accordingly. So I don't suddenly arrive and find I can't make a shot because the sun isn't in the right position.

We spent three days looking for locations. I came back with a complete photographic chart of the various locations, which I discussed with Warren. Then we determined the specific buildings we would use.

Once the buildings were chosen, they were matched up with the appropriate wardrobe and hair style and make-up changes, so that going into the still shooting, we knew where each would be shot, what the people would be wearing and what props would be used. Everything was determined in advance.

scene 10

This old library in Danbury (*scene 12*) was built in 1932, I believe. You can see Kipp's hairpiece!

This is an old gas station (*scene 10*) with a car we hired. All of the wardrobe here was selected from Eaves. I tried to choose poses that would accentuate certain youthful qualities; there's tension in the way Kipp is standing by the car. Actually he's holding himself in a way to cover up some beef he had accumulated. A lot of these clothes did not fit at all; his sweater is really six times too small. He really couldn't even wear the damn thing,

scene 14

scene 17

scene 19

scene 20

but he's sucking everything in. There's a great deal of angularity here — a more youthful way of handling one's self, as opposed to a *klutz*.

This wedding picture (*scene 14*) was done at an actual church. Those are all film extras in the background. All their wardrobe — not much that you can see — was selected in advance at Eaves. I feel it's very important to *select* your extras — never simply put out an extra call. It involves cost; you do get into the casting fee required by the union. But the end result pays off; the texture that extras give the final film is very much worth the time and the money.

This shot (*scene 17*) was completely propped, it was done in the Fall. The entire house was dressed for snow; artificial snow on the roof, bed sheets on the lawn, snow on the bushes from spray cans. We took a regular motion picture crew with us, with a full trailer truck, props, grips, the whole works. The only difference was we were using Kodak still cameras, as opposed to a Mitchell or an Arriflex.

One thing that contributed to the fine performance of the people in the commercial — I include the stills — and that made my job a great deal easier, was the suggestible nature of the commercial itself. When we were making the stills, Kipp would spend the morning being eighteen, the afternoon being forty-five. The next morning he would be twenty-six again, and the following day he might be nineteen. He kept bouncing from age to age.

Kipp normally wears glasses. At one point — when he was a younger man in the stills — he made the remark, "I'll be damned! I really feel I can see better." The power of suggestion of the situation, and the way he was made up, were strong enough to create that kind of feeling in an actor as seasoned as Kipp.

So I think a large part of the result was due to the suggestibility of the material we were working with. It's to the actors' credit that both of them could fall into it so easily, and let it control their feelings.

My main contribution with the stills was to provide the context, enough detail, real-enough costumes and wardrobe and real-enough situations to allow them to feel something. You can't create a specific feeling just by telling someone to do something in any particular way. You can make minor suggestions as to how they should smile or move or hold their body. Or you can talk about what the conditions of their life might be in this particular situation. But basically, if you provide enough detail, the actors draw from it and give back a great deal.

The little boy's haircut (*scene 19*) was given to him on the spot. We shaved the side of his head and parted his hair down the middle.

This is the Danbury railway station. (*scene 20*) Here we padded Kipp out again a little bit with body padding, to give him a little added weight.

scene 22

scene 24

scene 34A

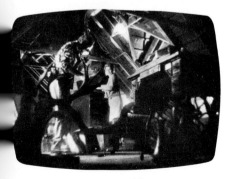

scene 2

We spent about half an hour rubbing that boy (*scene 22*) in the dirt; kicking him around a bit.

This (*scene 24*) is probably closest to Sarah's and Kipp's real ages, I suppose. Maybe a little older. I'm not sure. I got so confused during the filming, I never really knew. I'm even surprised when I meet Sarah now. It was all a great deal of fun — and some confusion.

I worked with the lab man developing these stills. I chose the shape each picture was to be, what kind of stock it was to be put on, what kind of edges — straight or serrated — how they were to be stained; whether glossy or matte, stiff or not stiff. On the wedding picture, I cut out that circle and put some little gold foil around the edge. All of those things were handcrafted in the darkroom. We spent a full day and night in the darkroom, just processing the still photographs.

The next step on location was to select a house exterior for the motion picture photography. We found it (*scene 34A*) in Danbury, right near the site of most of the stills. We took photographs of the outline of the roof. The interior shape of the attic was then determined by the exterior contour of the actual location house; the shape of the turret, the peak of the roof, the chimney, all in correct relationship to the real house. (*scene 2*)

Although producers don't always agree with me, I have a feeling about detail which may seem somewhat irrational. Even when detail is there but not seen, I still feel it definitely contributes something to the overall texture of the completed film. It's hard to say why; I think there are many things in filmmaking which really cannot be explained.

It's a necessity for me, many times, to feel the presence of that detail, in order to work properly on a set, or on a location. I also think it affects the actors. Sarah and Kipp can probably say something about that. I feel it helps the people; I know it helps me. It even helps the crew. It affects in intangible ways. The more unity you can create, the better the result.

Naturally, costs go up. That's another problem. On this particular set, we had a raised floor (*scene 2*) which means the cost went up $2,000 or $3,000. The MPO producer's first remark was "Do you really need a raised floor?" All you can do is mumble and drink your coffee. You try to worm your way out of it and get the raised floor, and still not be reckless about how you're spending money. All I can say is the amount of detailing obviously paid off; the reception the spot has received is not due to any one thing — it's due to a totality.

Sometimes you hear, "We paid for that whole wall, where the hell is it?", or, "We don't see the chest over in the corner that cost $500 to rent!" Those are the things that are fought over. Sometimes you win and sometimes you lose. In this case we won, a little bit.

In film you always go through stages. Putting down an abstract idea on paper requires certain adjustments. Realizing it in terms of a physical set requires other adjustments.

It suggests things that limit other things; and it also makes things possible you hadn't counted on. The three-dimensional emotional reality of your actors, moving within that set and dealing with one another, represents another adjustment; in terms of who they are, what they are, and what kind of "climate" they create within the set.

Another adjustment comes during editing, where other possibilities suggest themselves. At every step of the way, every time you move from one step to another, you have to make constant adjustments.

My normal procedure when creating a set — since my background is in architecture and design — is to formulate a plan myself first; a rough idea of what I would like the configuration of the set to look like. I make a rough sketch of the shape of the room; an impression I have of what the place might "feel" like. Then I call in the art director, and begin to talk about it in more specific terms. I tell him the kind of feeling, the kind of detail I want. He makes his own sketches; I make modifications or accept what he's shown me. In this case, we had a scale model made up in cardboard*, so I could feel the physicality of the thing. The model was particularly helpful because the cost of the set was considerable. It was necessary to have it, before we actually committed building the set itself.

Once I have scale plans of the set, I begin to block out my shooting in advance, based on those floor plans. I begin by working out camera angles and blocking movements. I plan as carefully as possible, trying to allow myself flexibility during shooting, changing my approach completely if necessary. I think the freest things require the most planning, and are the most difficult to achieve. Any fool can be spontaneous.

In film, you cannot leave things to chance. You have to come in with a clear idea of what you want, allowing yourself the freedom to throw it out the window and start from scratch. But you must approach film with a very definite idea of what you want to do or see. In my case I carry it to an extreme. I block out shots very specifically.

I make drawings of all the dolly moves and camera moves and where the camera would be in various places. Once I do that, I discuss them with my cameraman, to see if there are things we have to watch out for or adjust on a technical level.

Gerry Hirschfeld, the cameraman on "Yesterdays," has shot "The Incident," "Fail Safe," "Goodbye, Columbus," and seven or eight other feature films. It's very satisfying to work with someone like Gerry, because you can ask for anything.

*See illustration, page 91. — *Ed*.

The big problem is knowing what to ask for. Someone like Gerry can be very difficult for a director unsure of where he's going, because Gerry's a very strong personality, a very strong technician, and a very strong artist. You have to know where Gerry's going, so he follows and doesn't lead you.

I say that to his credit. He really forces you to go further with yourself — he pushes you to a kind of greater professionalism.

Gerry's one of the few cameramen I've worked with in New York to whom a crew immediately responds. We've all been on sets with a lot of noise, technicians disappearing constantly. You call for a prop or a grip and nobody is around. With Gerry on set, those things don't happen. I've worked with him on location outside MPO, with local people. There's an instant recognition of where he's at, on a professional level.

During the shooting itself, a great deal of additional dialogue was improvised on the spot, but is not in the finished film. A lot of little funny lines were not cut into the final film, as a result of decisions outside of my control.

Also, I do not agree with the kind of music eventually used. I would not use so sweet a rendition of that particular tune. I would have used a very different kind of recording, one that went against the obviousness of the situation; against the sentimentality of it. The song itself is sentimental, but I would have used a version that didn't cater to the situation we were creating, to give it a bit more tension. I would have had the song represent a happier quality and used more of the improvised dialogue as an undercurrent.

scene 42

The very end shot (*scene 42*) is not mine, either. It was tacked on later. I don't particularly agree with it. It's really against the feeling of the rest of the commercial and has no relationship to it. I think the decision to put the selection of snapshots on a brown table top is very bad. It's out of character.

I think it's all right to make these criticisms, because there are always disagreements in finishing; such as how a thing should be played, etc. I even felt there could even have been some sharper editing inside the attic itself.

THE CINEMATOGRAPHER

Gerald Hirschfeld, Vice-president and Director of Photography at MPO Videotronics, Inc., was the cinematographer and lighting director on "Yesterdays." Since that time, as Mike Cimino has indicated, Mr. Hirschfeld has become deeply involved in feature film production, and his past and recent "Director of Photography" credits include "Fail-Safe," "Goodbye, Columbus," "The Incident," "Last Summer," "Cotton Comes to Harlem," "Mastermind," and "Diary of a Mad Housewife."

A native of New York City, Mr. Hirschfeld attended Columbia University; then became a free-lance still photographer. A hitch with the Signal Corps during World War II converted him to motion-picture photography. In the early 50's, he began a busy career in television commercial photography — at which time he shot the first commercial the Editor of this book ever produced, followed by perhaps a thousand others.

Here Mr. Hirschfeld recalls both the simple and complicated cinematographic problems involved in getting "Yesterdays" onto motion-picture film:

It's a bit difficult — two years or more after we started on "Yesterdays" — to remember how it all began, and where I became involved with it. Perhaps it was just a chance meeting in the hall with Mike Cimino, when he said, "We've got a good one to do," or it may have been a formal production meeting at which we all sat down together. But once you're involved with Mike on a job, you *stay* involved, and you work on it until it's finished. Because of the way Mike works, it intrudes on much of your thinking. He's thorough, takes a lot of pains with preparation, and tries — and succeeds — in being very creative. One's thinking processes get to work at an early stage in Mike's productions.

One of the first photographic things we did were the still pictures. Somewhere along the line I became intrigued with the idea of shooting some of them with an original old Eastman Kodak folding camera. I remembered that the large roll film used with some of these cameras used to produce a picture the size of a postcard. I don't think any camera now — except a modern Speed Graphic, which requires cut film or a film pack — creates a picture that size.

We found an old camera, had it cleaned, polished up the lens, and fortunately were able to find some old-style Kodak Verichrome Film to use with it. The pictures turned out very well. The "formal" still photographer

scene 17

scene 33

scene 2

was shooting with his cameras while I was making with the folding Kodak. I felt like an old-time sightseer on a movie set. I also took Polaroid shots. For logistical reasons — it was important to see our color still results *before* the crew left the location — the snapshots in Scenes 22 and 24 I verified with a color Polaroid.

As you heard, what was unusual about the still shooting was that our crew went out with full motion picture equipment. The first set-up was to create that winter scene in the middle of the summer (*scene 17*) at the old house in Danbury. We used prop snow, white sheets, fake icicles — all the production paraphernalia that would go into shooting a motion picture film — *except* the motion picture camera. It was an unusual situation for me to be more or less standing by. I was very happy to have the old folding Kodak in my hands; it made me feel I was also being creative.

We tried to select sites and make our stills during times of day most advantageous in terms of light. We used reflectors to fill in the shadowed side, so that later reproduction of the stills — which had to be rephotographed and became, in a sense, "dupes" in the final commercial — would not be excessively contrasty. The reflectors helped a lot, by filling in the shadows.

Mike and Warren took great pains with the costumes and the backgrounds; I was mostly involved in checking make-up and hair, to be sure we were "aging" our actors as naturally as possible. Our make-up artist, Andy Ciannella, did a fantastic job. Our actors looked natural at all stages of the story; they looked the age they should have looked. They made a great contribution themselves in the way they posed, and by their general attitude. Actually, there was nobody involved with this production who did not contribute in some manner to creating a final great product.

At one point, there was some discussion about filming in an actual location attic. While this might have been possible, it would have been very restrictive on the director. Mike likes to move a camera; I like to light a set properly. On location, anything *can* be photographed — but the decision to use either a location or a studio rests on the final effect you desire, the camera movement you need, whether you are shooting sound, and the lighting problems.

For one thing, we had interior-to-exterior shots of the attic. (*scene 33*) This could have been done on location; we would have erected "parallels"* outside an attic window, and actually filmed through the window.

But other shots called for a very low camera position, dollying across the floor. (*scene 2*) This would have been practically an impossibility in a real attic, or at least very limited by the pitch of the roof and the eaves. Actually, our camera was outside the set area on those shots.

*Module scaffolding. — *Ed.*

scene 1A

scene 2

scene 6

A request was made that the entire set be elevated. This gave us a few practical steps for the actors to walk up or down, but more than that, I was able to keep my camera on a dolly with a very low vantage point. We could shoot through old sewing machines, old baskets, tables and chair legs for interesting effects.

Working with a director like Mike is always stimulating. His ideas stir new ones in my own mind. A thought or style he wants to create becomes a challenge, or many times can suggest a string of events that turn something like "Yesterdays" into a beautiful end product.

At some point, I suggested that to create the feeling of mustiness in an unused attic room whose bright windows contrasted with a low level of interior light, perhaps a "fog filter" over the camera lens would soften and mute the colors somewhat, and also add to the ever-present feeling of dust (in fact, in the opening shot, the actor blows quite a cloud of dust off the box he finds with the old snapshots in it). (*scene 1A*) This filter helped carry out that dusty feeling throughout the entire shooting — so you didn't just have dust on one shot with the other shots crystal clear. That would have been like opening with a master shot of a landscape on an overcast day, and when you go to shoot the closeups, you're in bright sunshine. It would be obvious something was amiss, even though the shots in themselves might be beautiful. So I did keep a fog filter over the camera lens for practically all the shooting in the attic.

Working with Karl Hueglin in the planning stage, I realized I would need light sources that would not only create a mood, and light the actors, but would also give credence to the set itself — reasons for light streaking across beams, etc. So we placed several windows strategically, with the bare bulb in the center of the attic serving as the apparent prime light source. (*scene 2*) Then the windows in the background gave a *reason* for strong close-up edge lighting. It gave a more dramatic feeling to the entire attic, which had to be rather dimly lit, yet still had to be seen in TV transmission without losing the feeling of our set.

This gets to be one of the more difficult problems of working in mood — or night — photography. Your levels of *key* light have to create the desired mood, with enough *fill* light to permit the viewer to know where he is and not wonder where somebody is in the background — someone who has to be seen even if he's a silhouette.

I made several shots from a ladder with a hand-held camera, some of them from high angles where raising a larger camera to the proper over-the-shoulders vantage point was impractical, due to the pitch of the roof and the size of the large camera magazines. (*scene 6*) I also did a walking shot, hand-held, following the actress up the stairs.* Used at the right time,

*This shot was left on the cutting-room floor. See George Fineman, p. 52. — *Ed.*

a hand-held camera imparts, of itself, a special mood to a cinematographic scene. Not being locked down to a half-ton of iron gives the camera a mobility and flexibility that even the best camera operator, working a smoothly-moving gear head, can't get; the camera can pan and tilt,* but it's still on a rock-steady position. Hand-held cameras can make moves that dolly-mounted cameras cannot. The hand-held camera we used added to the general informal feeling of "Yesterdays."

At many places, I huddled with Mike Cimino to discuss some point of photography or action or camera set-up. The commercial as it stands is evidence that our discussions led to a very happy level of creativity and artistic success. Above all, "Yesterdays" explicitly proves something I've felt as long as I have been working in this business; that there are so many demands to meet in the creation of an intelligent and artistic commercial that it is really impossible for it to be the "product" of any one person. And when *everybody* gets involved, and "puts out," with their interest stirred by the director and the agency producer, the product is usually something everyone can be proud of.

THE ACTORS

Sarah Meade, the Grandmother in "Yesterdays," is a very successful summer stock, New York theatre, television and TV commercial actress — who works her way for Kodak from a blonde co-ed to a grayhaired lady in less than 60 seconds. Born in Philadelphia, Miss Meade holds a B.A. in Theatre from Bennington College. She has appeared opposite such theatre luminaries as Burgess Meredith, Paul Muni, Hume Cronyn and Walter Matthau. Her professional career began in Dublin and Paris theatres, performing American repertory; her Broadway debut was in "Inherit the Wind."

Michael "Kipp" Currie — Grandpa — is an equally distinguished theatre and television actor. Born in Kingston, N.Y., he attended St. Lawrence University and the University of Iowa, and then taught college for a year near Kingston before embarking on his second career. Since 1965, Mr. Currie has lived with his family in Maine, flying to New York for professional assignments.

It is Mr. Currie's attic rummaging in "Yesterdays" that uncovers the dusty box of snapshot memories to set the commercial in motion. Here Sarah and Kipp discuss the personal experience of working for Mike Cimino:

*See "Storyboard Glossary," p. 162.

Obviously, it was very exciting for me. As an actress, you don't often get a chance to be in a commercial like this.

The thing that stands out more than anything else is the detail Mike mentioned, even before we went on location. I've never seen a commercial so meticulously and beautifully worked out ahead of time. It was fun, believe me.

The still shots were probably the most fun. We were forty in the morning and twenty-five in the afternoon. I spent a great deal of the time in the make-up chair or under a hair dryer, so I think Mike has overestimated my contribution. I really just did what I was told — put on the clothes and sat in a chair.

I didn't use a hairpiece at all. We had a remarkable woman who did my hair — Betty DeStefano. She could make it look long, short, curly, straight, or parted in the middle. She really did extraordinary work without any help from a hairpiece, and she did it quickly. Andy Ciannella, the make-up man, also did marvelous work; I enjoyed being fussed over and having someone change my face back to eighteen or nineteen.

*   *   *

It was a happy and satisfying experience to be a part of "Yesterdays." An actor works from the knowledge that he was picked for a role because of his quality and particular talents. This is his security; he hopes he will be used and not misused because of them. Whatever my quality, this was the first time I have ever been chosen to play in the same script the man as teen-ager, father and grandfather! But with the security and knowledge that I was cast correctly, the only one who could use or misuse me was the director.

Directors often speak of the temperamental actor. Yet the actor works with many, many directors, and might have his own ideas about them. On set, the actor senses almost immediately whether or not the production company, cameraman and agency people have come to a final decision as to how they want their commercial done. Any "lack of concept" affects the actor. While the director is telling the actor one thing, someone from the agency is whispering something else. That's why the actor insists on receiving direction from one source . . . the director.

Above all, the actor senses the *security* of the director; does the director know himself, his job and how to achieve his goal? Rather than restricting the actor, does he allow the actor to try it his way (within reason), and thus let the particular quality the actor was picked for in the first place come through? This doesn't mean the actor is given carte blanche, but the secure actor working with a secure director creates a believable result.

When everyone seems to know what they are doing and feels their own special contribution, it cannot help but make a difference in the final product. On location, this becomes even more important. Every evening after shooting, George Marvin, the MPO Assistant Director, went to every member of the cast and crew to report where people were meeting that night, to relax or whatever. A simple courtesy, but one all too often neglected. I have known cases where actors, after a day's shooting, were actually left behind at the location because they had been forgotten! The atmosphere of "Yesterdays," however, was one of friendliness and cooperation.

I was interested in what Sarah just said about being made up and shot: "I really did just what I was told — put on the clothes and sat in a chair." This was very true about the still work; I had never done any before. Maybe because of this, and because I am basically an actor, the still work became a weird and wonderful experience. Let alone the challenge to Andy Ciannella!

scene 10

It was a shock, standing in the set, and then turning to see a modern camera and the modern rushing 20th Century outside. At each change in age, I found myself going back in time and experiencing the whole atmosphere, feelings and attitudes of the 1930s. I must say that the detail certainly contributed: it was a shock to be by a gas station in early clothes with full head of hair, standing by that great old car. (*scene 10*) It reached a point where I was sitting in the car, reading a newspaper, waiting for the set to be finished. We were "being" nineteen or so. Then I realized I wasn't wearing my glasses to read . . . *and did not when I was nineteen!*

With "Yesterdays," everything seemed to jell. It was well thought out, had a great creative, *secure* director in Mike, and pleasant and thoughtful people to work with. One hated to leave that attic set. I only wished we were doing a full-length film instead.

NOTE: The questions and discussion that followed this presentation appear on p. 140 ff.

5
Pre-Production
&
Casting

THE PRODUCER

"I've never seen a commercial so meticulously and beautifully worked out ahead of time," said Sarah Meade. It is true that a two-minute "story" commercial like "Yesterdays" requires a huge amount of pre-planning. Unlike many of the psychedelic, spastically-edited 30-second commercials now on the air, "Yesterdays" represented a true "mini-movie," Hollywood-style.

But besides requiring such pre-planning, "Yesterdays" truly received it — in extra measure. Perhaps those participating in the project anticipated the non-ephemeral nature of this particular production, and synergistically, offered their very best from the very beginning.

Warren Aldoretta traces some of those first planning steps:

You may have the idea that the actual filming of a commercial is more creative and more exciting than the pre-production planning. Not really true at all.

Let me comment briefly on storyboards. The way our Thompson group works on Kodak, the storyboard is never an instrument that locks us into our shooting. It is merely a "board of intent," used for discussion purposes and to allow a point of departure at meetings; only a frame of reference. Many times, by looking at a storyboard, a producer can find inherent traps in the script. But also consider the fact that Fellini has made as many as 150 thumbnail sketches for a single movie scene; and you get an idea how one small storyboard picture, done by a sketch artist to tie in one scene, is not a fully valid way to consider or describe a film. A storyboard thus serves as an important frame of reference, but not as a final shooting commitment.

When a producer begins to consider the many production companies available to him, he performs his major service to the client? How? What actually happens?

He deliberately breaks all existing rules and mentally sprouts wings. Out goes the book of "do's" and "don'ts," all the professional rules and regulations of what he can and cannot do. He fires up his creative imagination, and takes off on a creative exploration of the exciting work of available talent.

Every producer in the Kodak Group has access to a bird's-eye view of the vast talent provided by all the production companies from coast to coast. We work hard to achieve this overview. A producer must be aware, for the client's sake if for no other reason, of all the talented people available to solve his particular problems at a specific time. He must always be able to look at creative talent and see it as a fluid thing, rather than isolated and pigeon-holed. We look for new combinations to penetrate new areas and bring new vitality to all our commercial ideas.

In my case, coming from an art direction background, I am constantly reminding myself that I am first and foremost an advertising man. Advertising is selling the client's product; and selling, like politics, is based on the power of persuasion. This power of persuasion is an intuitive art — not found in books and not easily learned.

There is another area I feel very strongly about, an area that ties in closely with the power of persuasion; an area that makes a commercial compelling, that motivates you to buy. I am talking about picking the right actor through effective casting, an area that is a specialty unto itself. Casting must be right on target. I don't care how strong an idea or its execution is, if we do not have a cast that can relax and improvise in front of a camera and make things happen, we are in big trouble.

Mike Cimino paid our casting department a very wonderful compliment. He mentioned that the talent on "Yesterdays" was so good, he felt all he had to to do was point them in a certain direction and they themselves went back into the experience of their own lives and came up with improvised lines in the attic. That lets you realize just how good those people really were.

About two years ago, I came across a little description of the word "wonder." I jotted it down in a notebook. Every once in a while I refer to it:

Wonder is a choice quality expressed by the creative person. It sees the shine and beauty of being, everywhere. It refuses to let any task drop to the level of the mundane, the colorless, the monotonous. Wonder sees infinity. It never gets familiar with smallness, or with voids. It knows only expanding horizons.

There is great food for thought in those few lines. How can we interpret them to increase our awareness and judgment? I would say, through touching the lives of other people, working closely with people in clubs and in groups, getting enthusiastic about the theatre, about ballet, about concerts, and sports, getting together with a group and discussing the latest films, reading books, trade publications and foreign magazines, listening to music and voice on the radio, studying television and covering fashion shows, stopping at the Museum of Modern Art, making frequent visits to Greenwich Village, and taking lots of time to look at production house sample reels and video tape. In short, caring and wondering . . . wondering . . . wondering about the world around us.

You may think this all sounds "very groovy"; when do we find time for all this conscious exposure? The answer to that question may surprise you. As an individual you simply cannot do it; but as a member of a group you can, provided the group is designed and structured to allow a free exchange of thoughts and ideas.

The Kodak production team at Thompson under Granger Tripp, is headed by Raymond Fragasso, who encourages just that type of spirit. Ray is a turned-on guy who gets very involved with today's creative scene.

He encourages all of us to share ideas and experiences; this, in turn, allows each of us to gain an overall understanding of the latest happenings in the business.

After every shooting, for example, we get together as a group for an exchange of experiences that have happened on location. This constant flow and unfoldment helps us all to grow, particularly because we are working with suppliers from all over the world.

Our good client Ted Genock, from Kodak, has also done much to make us aware of new developments in this business. He is constantly calling up about a new helicopter rig, or a new 3-D projection screen, or what have you. This type of enthusiasm is part of the secret of our success. Here are some concrete examples of how it works:

A little over two years ago, a "snorkel" camera was developed at Princeton. While shooting a Kodak job on the Coast, Ray met Chris Peterson, and from him learned the potential in the "snorkel" idea. He set up a screening for our Group, soon followed by a commercial idea, and a client "O.K." to shoot using this new technique in California.

When Expo '67 exploded into a film fair, Ray met again with one of the key designers of the multiple-image school. Then he ran critical tests, using the multiple-image principle and reducing it to a 21″ television screen.

Shortly thereafter, we were shooting the Kodak commercial "Omnibus," based on the multiple-image concept. This gives an idea, I think, of how Ray's philosophy pays off.

So the producer floats around for a while in this blue-sky world of creative combinations; then finally sends a message back to ground control at Thompson. He contacts the Cost Estimator. They discuss the basic feeling and approach he has in mind, and go to work to provide a realistic evaluation in dollars and cents. Now the producer performs another important duty to the client — he comes back down to economic ground.

This requires a great deal of discipline, because we are talking about two completely opposite forces. The creative area is a scintillating, free-swinging type of thing, generating an abundance of emotion in the individual. But he has also to make certain that what he plans to do is not just an exciting package, but one that is sound and practical as well.

The Cost Estimator wipes the steam off the producer's heat shield and gives him a radar fix, a very professional frame of reference in dollars and cents that allows selection of at least three production companies to bid on the commercial.

As we go through these bidding sessions, the Cost Estimator attends each meeting, working very closely with the producer on the entire development of the concept. There's one very important thing that has to happen; each production company must be given exactly the same information, so they can bid according to the same ground rules. This is mandatory for controlling the entire bidding approach.

On numerous occasions, I have seen Ray Fragasso put on his dollar-value hat to hold a duel with Sel Shillinglaw, our Cost Estimator at Thompson. To watch this is a unique experience. Ray is a free-swinging creative talent, but at the same time he is professional enough to come to real grips in the area of dollars and cents. Even though there may be thousands of dollars involved, he and the Cost Estimator usually come out the other end within two or three hundred dollars of each other. That's always impressed me.

THE ESTIMATOR

Selwyn Shillinglaw is Commercial Production Cost Estimator at J. Walter Thompson Co. Born in the Midwest and a design and photography graduate of the Art Institute of Chicago, Mr. Shillinglaw worked first for Sarra, Inc., the Chicago photographers, and then went overseas to continue his study of art. Upon his return, he joined Sarra's New York television studios as production manager, and worked there for seven years.

A brief stint as producer/cost estimator at Filmex in New York preceded Mr. Shillinglaw's move to Thompson in 1965. Here he comments on the procedures followed in "costing out" the "Yesterdays" commercial for final client budget approval:

Thompson is unique. We are big. We actually have five creative agencies going. Each is a sizable group in itself, so we are in a position to have service facilities other agencies do not enjoy. My job is one. I am somewhat unique in my field; there are only two or three guys like me in the advertising business.

First, I have decided not to discuss the cost of this commercial. There are good reasons for this. It was done over two-and-a-half years ago. Union rates have increased a couple of times since then, and they will continue to increase on a sliding scale. Also, we went a day over estimate in still photography, and six hours over estimate in the live photography. MPO could not reproduce that commercial today for the same price they originally quoted.* So we can't use the price as a judgment, since the spot cannot be duplicated the same way.

Warren mentioned our "relaxed" storyboards and scripts. I want to touch on that a bit, too, because I think it an interesting approach, and unique to certain types of advertising. Kodak does it; our Ford and Pan Am people often do it. Even if there is a storyboard, it rarely is shown to the production company or to the director considered for the job. This is to try to get a much looser and more flexible reaction from production talent whom we are considering using; it does not lock them into any preconceived image. This is the way most of Kodak's things are done, including "Yesterdays."

I was introduced to this spot in September, 1966. After talking to Warren, it became obvious we had a two-minute film. It looked as if it would require at least two days of live photography — probably one day

---

*A 1970 bid on a similarly-constructed commercial might approach $70,000. — *Ed.*

in the studio and just enough live photography outdoors to make another day. There would be a couple of days of still photography involved. We worked this out in our own minds before we talked to any suppliers.

Then we got into the other area Warren was talking about, one we explored very freely on this particular project. We talked to eight companies — five or six more than we usually consider. Warren was going deeply into creative exploration, checking directorial reaction to the commercial.

One very successful company here in New York declined to bid because they didn't think the script offered much potential; they did not want to be involved in a project that didn't appear to offer much of an idea. One company was very expensive — they are no longer in business. One company came within the realm of the lowest bidder, projecting a very different attitude to the production; they hoped to shoot the whole thing on location in Vermont. The rest of the suppliers were all within 4% of my original estimate, which is a pretty good score. The supplier we finally settled on, MPO, was not the low bidder. They were in the middle of that 4% range, roughly within 3% of my original estimate.

At Thompson, servicing all accounts as I do gives me an opportunity to keep a free exchange going with suppliers; a pretty accurate knowledge of their costing procedure, their mark-up procedure. All groups at Thompson benefit from this knowledge. This also gives me a realistic approach to costing out the original estimate. It saves a great deal of heartache if we know that when whatever we want to do is unrealistic, we can go back, rewrite the script, and start over again. It also saves repeating all that procedure with a lot of suppliers, because making an estimate is an expensive thing. As far as the production house is concerned, the people who estimate are some of the most expensive people in the company; if you consider it on the basis of salary, an estimate probably can run from one to several hundred dollars to make, yet this is something they have to offer free. So we save money for the production company, and we save embarassment to ourselves.

THE CASTING DIRECTOR

Evelyn Barnes Pierce is in charge of the Casting Department at J. Walter Thompson Co. — a group of thirteen people to whom TV production turns when they require commercial talent. Miss Pierce grew up in Illinois, holds a B.A. from Wellesley, and studied acting with Maria Ouspenskaya and directing and playwriting at the New School in New York City.

Miss Pierce seems like a fixture at Thompson (she has been their Casting Director for fifteen years), yet it is her second career that followed quite a busy success in the theatre. In that first career, Miss Pierce started as a radio actress and writer, became National Casting Director of the WPA Federal Theatre, served as Casting Director of the Theatre Guild, and directed on- and off-Broadway and summer stock plays, revues and ballet. Through casting and producing for the growing television medium, Miss Pierce came into advertising, and worked at a succession of advertising agencies — BBDO, Compton, Kenyon & Eckhardt, and Fuller, Smith & Ross — before moving to Thompson.

As Thompson's Casting Director, Miss Pierce must know not only who is good for a certain role — she must know who is best. But her basic recommendations are still multiple; final decisions are usually left to the producer and his commercial director:

When Warren was talking about the way people, in a larger sense, "prepare" themselves, I began thinking about what we try to do in the Casting Department. Many lunchtimes I'll nip over to the Museum of Modern Art and look at a Picasso sculpture exhibit, or toot up to see a little Klee at the Guggenheim.

In our department we get in before nine, and talk when we first get in. Someone's read a book, or is all het up about a political candidate; these are wonderful sessions.

I head a department whose chief *raison d'être* is to service the Agency. This department began about sixteen years ago and now has 12,500 people in a master talent file. Most of them have been interviewed; all have been categorized and cross-filed. This master file never leaves the Casting Department. The ground work that one should properly take for granted does exist, and we call upon it in many different ways. In order to assemble this file of 12,500 talents, we go everywhere. To La Mama. To Lincoln Center. To the theatre as much as possible (off-Broadway, off-off-Broadway, on Broadway) — every place where we can see the live actor in all stages of development.

You know how desperate schools are for people to talk to graduating classes. Even though they are nice enough to ask if you have time, the only reason I go is that these are the reservoirs of talent to come. If you can help them with some realistic point of view about our business, in the end it helps you. Once one trudges over to the American Academy of Dramatic Arts, or the High School for Performing Arts, to chat with these kids, they let you know when they do whatever they do, and you keep in touch with them. In our business we tend to become much too specialized. We get to be such bores; everytime you go out, you talk about what you do. And if what you do is highly departmentalized, you become a bore. So the thirteen of us try to keep abreast of things, to function as well as we can for people like Warren. We can go to the reservoir; we should.

It is a pleasure to talk now about the Kodak experience. To work with the Kodak group is a special plus. They communicate. They listen to ideas; they talk and you can listen. Without that kind of real communication, you get what you pay for: if you get talent calls that are very skimpy, that's what you give in return. Not so with the Kodak people, however. Warren's pattern is always to be specific; the minute he could brief us, help us, start us thinking, he did.

He strolled in one day and said, "Hey, here's something kind of interesting." We sat down and talked right then about actors, not models, who might be suitable. We wound up with them in Kipp Currie and Sarah Meade (only today I noticed that they were both on Broadway together in "Inherit the Wind.")

Talking with Warren, you don't need storyboards — you never do if you're talking to a good producer. When there is truly an exchange, he starts you thinking, and then you use all the resources you have. First we thought we might want to cast a real honest-to-goodness family, though it seldom if ever works that way. Like all mystique in the theatre, if you *make* it, it's better than if it's *real*. This way you also have control over the end product. That's what we ended up doing, of course. I won't bore you with all the long discussions of approaches, production meetings and so forth.

When we got into gear it took us — thank God for Warren again — only a week of casting, because we had been given time to be prepared. We had six casting sessions for "Yesterdays." We saw 113 people; 12 others we were very anxious to bring to Warren's attention were not available, as often happens. We had to find the mother, father, two sons, and one son's wife and her son.

We went through the usual long discussions, pre-production meetings and so forth. Thank God, again, for Warren, because he gave us time to prepare, time to think — even time to pre-screen people whom we had not seen for a while (because we hate to waste the producer's time — sometimes we do, but we try not to). After several days of beating the bushes, screening and selecting — discussing all the while and keeping close to Warren — we began a week of casting. On the first day we chose Kipp, on the fifth day Sarah, and on the sixth day we chose the little grandson. He was three years old then; I hear he has since retired from the business. I guess he was really a star. (*scene 37*) That was our casting timetable.

We did the still photography first, for "preventive" reasons. The SAG Code is not clear whether *still* photography represents the beginning of

scene 37

"principal photography." Once the cameras start, you must pay the performer for each day regardless of whether he is called or not. That is one of the really minus aspects of the Code, negotiated back in 1953 in the first SAG negotiation in the East. This "continuous employment" provision was really designed for feature films; it has no relevance to commercials at all. But we're stuck with it.

To avoid any problems of continuous employment and having to pay actors on call whether required or not, and thus down the drain, we did our still photography first. After one week of casting and one week of shooting, the filming was completed.

THE STYLIST

Since leaving Columbus, Ohio, Joyce Hsu, Fashion Coordinator at J. Walter Thompson Company, has alternated her career between the worlds of fashion and broadcasting. Miss Hsu's first job was with the National Broadcasting Company. Then she moved to Vogue Magazine as an editorial assistant, and from there to Harper's Bazaar as Assistant Fabric Editor.

At Thompson, her job is to make on-camera talent look fashionable — but with "Yesterdays," her task was considerably more complicated:

Thompson's Fashion Department employs five stylists, plus the Fashion Director. She works on all accounts, primarily in the area of fashion styling for commercials and ads. The Director also works on fashion tie-ins, using fabric and color forecast reports; talks about beauty and make-up.

We are primarily concerned with contemporary and even advanced fashions. We keep up with the latest in everything to do with fashions, by attending shows, reading, and by keeping our eyes open as to what is happening in the stores and on the streets. Our usual procedure in the production of a commercial, upon receiving the script or storyboard, is to discuss with the producer and/or director the wardrobe for the cast, bearing in mind the sub-colors, the talent types or images, and what they should look like. Is the woman supposed to look like a housewife, a high-fashion model, or what? Next we make a selection of the required wardrobe, either using outside resources or our own Thompson wardrobe, or choosing from the actor's own wardrobe. Then we schedule a fitting, for the producer's approval. The final choice is made and completely accessorized before production.

Just prior to being assigned to "Yesterdays," I had worked on another commercial that went back to approximately the same time period. Going to past issues of *Vogue* in the Condé Nast library, I made notes of prevalent silhouettes, lengths of skirts, hair styles, make-up, shoes, and all other accessories. Even though I would not be directly responsible for hair and make-up (Andy Cianella and Betty De Stefano did excellent jobs, as you've heard), it is always better to know the right look from head to toe, and not just clothing. With a little review, then, I was pretty well set with styles for these periods. There were a total of thirty-one complete wardrobe outfits for the complete cast — counting extras and the infant.

Then Warren and Mike determined what should be worn in each scene. After obtaining the names of the actors from casting and getting their sizes, I was able to search for the costumes. My first choice for a costume house turned out to be my main source: Costume Associates, who worked closely with us throughout the entire production, and last minute changes. They supplied twenty of the costumes. Mike mentioned going to Eaves: the wedding gowns for the 1938 wedding scene were not so good at Costume Associates; I found several good ones at Eaves which I reserved for Mike and Warren to see.

I made several selections and met Warren, Mike, Gayle Carlisle (our Fashion Director) and Karl Hueglin at the fashion house one afternoon, to review the selection. That meeting lasted until 10:00 p.m. We selected the costumes to be used, the changes, the additions, the accessories. Each costume was completely correct to the minutest detail, including the number of buttons on the sleeves or the pearl necklace, or the right pin.

Sarah Meade had a total of five hours' fittings on two different days. Kipp Currie had three-and-a-half hours of fittings on two different days. All fittings were with Warren and Mike present. All of the other members of the cast had fittings for their wardrobe — even the extras. These fittings averaged half-an-hour each.

Ev Pierce mentioned a week for casting and a week for production. Add to that the week for fashion. We had fashion in undergarments, too. I had to make Kipp look younger. Sarah wore a flattening brassiere, because of the flatchested '30's look, and a waist cinch to make her look younger. Kipp also wore a cinch.

Looking for accessories led me to places I had not ventured before. Silk stockings were the fashion of the Thirties; at the suggestion of Eleanor Knowles, I went down to the Bowery and found them at Phil's Hosiery, a little place there. For open-toed Joan Crawford-type shoes, and wing-tipped men's shoes, I went to the Salvation Army store on the West Side.

Even though Costume Associates supplied most of the costumes, we used a total of sixteen outside resources, plus some items from the Thompson wardrobe, and even the actor's own wardrobe, to complete all the costumes needed for this commercial. The dress and sweater Sarah wore in her attic scene belong to her.

Although most of a stylist's work is over before production, on the day of shooting, we also saw to it that the wardrobe was pressed and ready, and dressed the actors as each scene was ready to be shot. After the shooting was over, we cleaned up the wardrobe and returned it to the costume house. We sent Thompson wardrobes to the cleaners, and wrote a report on the wardrobe used and all the expenditures incurred.

THE SET DESIGNER

Karl Hueglin is a free-lance Scenic Designer who works extensively with MPO Videotronics, Inc. A New Yorker, he studied art at Columbia University and worked four years in summer stock. After U.S. Army service in Germany, he became involved in the early days of television scenic design, doing live dramatic shows for the DuMont Network. Off-Broadway, Mr. Hueglin designed the sets for "The Hostage" and "Billy Liar." He is directly responsible for the physical conception of the attic in "Yesterdays," with all its dusty mood and charm — and its wonderful Victorian props:

Is the designer's job something you shouldn't be aware of? Robert Edmond Jones once said the only way he knew if he did his job well was to go into the audience at intermission, and see if they just talked about how great the play was, without mentioning anything about the sets.

I always wonder if designers really feel like that. Sometimes, you like to feel you are being accepted for having done your job well.

Actually, the job of the designer or art director is sort of odd. You can compare it to being a decorator, except you end up *building* the structure. You can build anything from a tenement to a palace, interior or exterior. It is similar, yet has many variations.

My first contact with "Yesterdays" was when I met Warren and Mike in the hall at MPO, and Mike said something like, "I've got a great fun job for you," and that was the last I heard for quite a while. I work this way, on and off, with Mike; he gives me a little bit, and then runs away, because he's got a meeting with somebody else.

I have worked on Kodak for several years with many directors and many creative groups at Thompson. Recently they got much more creative. In the old days, you had to design "for the Midwest." I hope I am not saying anything wrong, but it got to be a little boring. There was nothing creative about it, except when we did the Photography Show once a year on Ed Sullivan, and had to copy some real wild displays some display company made in Chicago, recreating them in New York in order to film them with Sullivan.

With "Yesterdays," the next thing I heard about was a basement that somewhere along the line got changed to an attic. When we got down to discussing the reasons for the attic, I don't know who finally convinced the agency the attic was warmer and more interesting than a cold, dark, damp basement; you put more things in an attic. I always like to think I had something to do with it. I don't know.

I sat down with Mike and discussed the basic requirements he would need to stage and direct the job. He wanted a stairway with the action of Grandpa coming upstairs. He needed windows in all the walls, so that we would have "outside light" coming in, in addition to the interior light, just a bare light bulb.

As to props, in some cases you can be specific, but many times you just go out and look, and find whatever you can, because shapes mean more in this type of situation. You're looking for things that have a feeling of being of the period.

Of course we had "wild" (movable) walls which we had to be able to use in or out — in order to be able to light, and get the camera into different positions.

The original idea was for doing this in a real attic on location; but one of the problems was the amount of control. We had shots from outside inside — at the beginning of the commercial. (*scene 1A*) We had shots where we wanted the camera in positions we could not possibly get. And if you have gone through some Victorian attics (and I guess everybody has at one time or another), you realize it is almost impossible to get up there with a camera and the number of people required to do a decent job and have the right lighting. We wound up deciding to construct the attic.

The basic area was twenty-four feet square. My model (*page 91*) was made not to be beautiful, but to give Mike ideas to block his direction, and decide which elements had to be removable.

As for the interior of the set — a lot of it came from memory, things seen in the past, research I did after I got involved, including seeking locations for the still photographs.

At that point, after the model was made, I made a floor plan, again very simple. The plan gave the carpenter a rough layout of the areas involved. Mike approved this, and from then on it was merely a matter of getting the thing built.

For most stage construction by film producers and for television, you do not build a whole house. You build only what you see of it — the façade —

scene 1A

scene 6

scene 2

so the walls behind are unfinished. But for this commercial, we had to really build the whole attic from the floor up — rafters, all the interior sheathing, and the floor. The idea of putting down actual floorboards came because there are many scenes where you *see* the boards (*scene 6*) and an attic has spaces between boards; in 50 years, the wood shrinks. In some shots (*scene 2*) you will notice batten strips applied over 2′x8′ boards, which was the way they constructed houses forty or fifty years ago. We wanted to give an interior shingle effect, and yet not get into the expense of putting shingles on, or I would probably still be shingling right now. What we did instead was to stain and apply large sheets of 4′x8′ plywood, with the grain in them closely approximating the back of an aged shingle. Of course, by doing this, we were able to save the 4′x8′ sheets for future productions, and thus were able to help MPO's budget.

A set designer is supposed to be creative, yet he is also supposed to make the set fit into the magical little figure that the producer, Sel, and the film production house all want to come out with. Unfortunately there are many things you cannot control.

The entire set was built on a platform. (*scene 2*) We had to take the entire stage and build it three feet higher. There are no stages in New York with trap doors similar to theatre stages. This is something never done in a movie studio, where floor requirements are much more demanding for heavy camera dollies to move on.

After the carpenters got all the little complicated, compounded corners and everything fixed up, and the painters finished their job, the propping wound up being a tremendous amount of fun.

I had an excellent prop man working with me who had a great feel. You couldn't go to a normal prop house. First of all, you're looking for odd things, old trunks that are battered, old newspapers, old skis with the old bindings on them, books, old botles, everything you think you might find in an old Victorian attic.

Our biggest source for all this was "thrift shops." Forgetting the prop shops, we wound up looking in thrift shops all the way from here to Hempstead. We found fantastic things that weren't even necessary for the production, things I now have at home — a few little knick-knacks, and some great research books I just happened to find, looking through some old thrown-away things.

We wanted old papers. We found a group that one vendor just happened to have in the corner of his basement. They were all beautiful and brittle, but they wound up falling apart, so we decided to make our own paper. One way was to age it in an oven, but then it came back brittle again, so we finally wound up dying it. The brittle edges we created with heat; the overall color with dye.

Model of attic set

Another factor that sometimes isn't evident in the picture itself is that old-fashioned houses have rock-wool insulation blown into them, when they are renovated. Mike is extremely demanding in his realism; you make it real the first time, or you'll go back and do it again, even at 5:30 in the morning. I'm not complaining. I think it is more fun to know the direction you're going, and to go there in the first place, rather than hold back and do a half-baked job.

Mike wanted the back half of the attic to show exposed timbers, with actual rock-wool insulation. This made for a little more detail in the back; there were even scenes in which you could see it.

The final thing we did was to cover the whole place with dust and cobwebs. There was so much dust that when the actors walked, it billowed up. In the very first scene Grandpa blows dust off a pile of books he picks up. Well, I have a sore throat right now and I had a sore throat twice as bad all day long that day, because the entire studio was completely saturated with dust.

Joyce Hsu said she had to clean up after her job. I just try to walk away and somebody else sweeps up, and I'm thankful I'm not there to see what happens.

scene 1A

scene 34A

scene 2

scene 4

We wanted windows on each side. We wound up putting in a variety of windows. (*scene 1A*) This was on the camera-left side of the house. We wound up adding another window which you can see through. Then in the rear we had two windows which simulated the location we found, with a chimney up the side of the house and small windows on either side. Amazingly enough, the turret was adapted to our basic idea *before* we found the location, and then we looked for one in our location and found it! (*scene 34A*)

The attic beams were kept fairly low, so Mike would be able to get a wide shot; I believe the overall height from floor to ridge pole was ten feet. We wound up getting some old glass shades with scenes painted on them; kind of elaborate, but they gave us just the amount of interior light that we wanted.

This was an old sewing machine (*scene 2*), which means more in the actual film when you dolly by it. You vaguely see the lathing strips at the top, which create a shadow line. A lot of times in film, if that were just a plain area without the shadow line, it would look uninteresting — it would look like a studio set.

When I look at a set and see complicated things that are ridiculous for people to put on a set, I think it's probably real and shot on location. Of course, in this business, the compliment you should get is, "Gee, what location did you shoot it on?" People have said that about this commercial.

We decided the plastic brick didn't look right, so we did what you have seen in many older houses, where the pointing mortar just comes oozing out and dries there. (*scene 4*) In old attics, they didn't clean it up because it didn't show, though a more careful craftsman would clean it up. It made an interesting texture and changed the character of the brick.

Here are the dusty floor boards (*scene 6*). You can see the spacing between them. The records were old — out of someone's basement. Old cardboard boxes troubled us with the same brittleness we found with old paper. Yet it turned out to be more economical to use really old boxes, rather than spend hours making them old. The prop man found what we needed.

This is an interior-exterior shot (*scene 33*) Mike came up with at one point. I had faced the outside of this set so he could use it; he had said something about it in pre-production. While out shooting on Danbury location, he remembered, "I want to shoot an outside set shot." He had forgotten he had even told me about it. He called up New York and said "You've got to stay and fix the set." Luckily, it was already there.

NOTE: The questions and discussion that followed this presentation appear on p. 145

6
Agency Creation & Presentation

scene 6

scene 33

THE CREATIVE DIRECTOR

At this point, we have passed through all the technical problems of producing, distributing and airing "Yesterdays". Now we reach backwards to the moment when one individual — not a committee — gathered his brain cells together to develop a communicable marketing idea. And *then* said to his committee, "How do you like it?"

Perhaps one of the most interesting things about the development of "Yesterdays" is that the original idea — presented in script form by copywriter Ken Thoren on April 15, 1966 — was so strong that it suffered few of the sea changes that usually affect commercials in their voyage from idea to the face of the TV tube.

To the committee — an agency committee — Kodak had already said: "We like your media buy. We think we can use a two-minute commercial. This is the product we wish to push. What do you recommend for communicating with our potential customers in front of TV sets in Chicago, New York, Los Angeles — and Upper Snowshoe, Montana?"

In charge of Thompson's answer to that question was Granger Tripp, senior vice-president and one of the Agency's five creative directors. Kodak is one of his several account responsibilities. Mr. Tripp grew up in the New York suburbs, gained a B.A. from Union College in Schenectady, and in the early 1940's slipped into a broadcast advertising career through the same front door as the present Editor — by helping to found his college's radio station.

After two years in the U.S. Army, Mr. Tripp joined a radio advertising monitoring service, rising to the post of vice-president in charge of sales and public relations. After eight years in that job, he moved — in 1953 — to J. Walter Thompson Co. as a broadcast advertising writer. His vice-presidential stripes were won in 1960. Six years later he was made a creative supervisor, and is now a senior V.P. with creative responsibilities for a dozen prestigious Thompson accounts.

An important part of Mr. Tripp's job is maintaining a fertile agency creative climate to produce ideas like "Yesterdays;" then he has to nourish them, and help shape them into final advertising form. He asks first:

How is a commercial born?

It really begins of course, with a client problem, a marketing problem. How is information about this problem transmitted from the client to the people who create the commercial?

The role of the account representative is key in this. His importance is often overlooked. It is absolutely vital that information be transmitted clearly, accurately, and if possible, succinctly.

The creative people want to know all they possibly can about the product that is to be sold, where the market is, and who the people are to whom the commercial must appeal.

They will want to know what kind of a production budget they must work within. And they will want to know whether the commercial will be part of a campaign, whether it will appear as a spot or on a program, and if in a program, what kind, what the surrounding material will be like. All of this the group head and the writer, art director, and producer should know before they can go to work.

What the creative supervisor and his people hope is that the account representative will transmit the problem to them, and that he will not try to limit them to one solution. It is difficult if someone comes back from the client and says, "Here is what we want, a commercial just like so." We would rather have the account men let *us* propose a solution.

At this point it is the function of the group head or creative supervisor to turn the information over to the people who will do the actual writing.

Here he has a choice that will vary from agency to agency, group to group, occasion to occasion. He may assign the project to one individual, or he may turn it over to a writer/art director team, or a writer/art director/producer team. He may in some cases give the problem first to an ar director or first to a producer. It may be turned over to a whole group of writers, or just one.

Less often, I think, in the case of Kodak than with some other accounts, will we call in everybody and say, "Go off and think up thousands of ideas on this particular problem." We prefer instead to choose the best person for the job and make it his responsibility.

There is something to be said for competition within a group; something to be said for lots of ideas. But sometimes if you make a problem the responsibility of a dozen people, it becomes the responsibility of no one. As between the two methods of operation, generally I think it is better to leave the responsibility with one individual.

Again, the transmission of information is terribly important. It is not easy to tell the people involved everything they need to know, but this is the function of the group head or creative supervisor.

I have been speaking in generalities, because here as in so many other aspects of its creation, "Yesterdays" was an exception. We did not get a specific assignment from the client or have a specific meeting.

Essentially, "Yesterdays" was designed to promote the activity of picture-taking; designed to motivate people, to reinforce their knowledge that picture-taking is important, and to remind them of the many different occasions on which they ought to take pictures.

This is a continuing assignment. Back in 1966 when this commercial was written, Ken Thoren had already completed other outstanding commercials, aimed at the same basic problem. One of them appeared on our first Academy Awards Show. It was called, "The Way You Look Tonight," and was produced by Ray Fragasso. Another one, "Sunrise-Sunset" appeared on the second Academy Awards Show, and won the Grand Prix in Venice. So Ken was well aware of the need for this kind of commercial and simply created it as part of his continuing work on the Kodak account.

Let me skip over his part for a moment, just to continue the chain of events in the creation of a commercial. Once it is written or put on storyboards, it comes back to the group head, then to the account representative, and through them to the client.

What is important — and difficult — at this point, is summed up in a quotation from Leo Burnett that I can never remember verbatim. He said something like: *"Lots of people can create good advertising, but it takes a real genius to keep his hands off a good ad when he sees one."*

The function of a group head when he sees a commercial like "Yesterdays" or "Sunrise-Sunset" is to keep his cotton-picking hands off it. That applies to everyone else who touches the commercial in its path from creation to client approval, and admittedly, it is hard. *It is difficult to keep your hands off any advertising.*

There are times when changes are essential, but I think it is significant that the basic concept of "Yesterdays" was so strong, it survived from script through storyboard to finished commercial with no major changes. What is very unusual among commercials is any resemblance of its initial script to the finished commercial.

THE WRITER

Kenneth A. Thoren has been with J. Walter Thompson Company for eight years, currently as a vice-president and copy group head. His Kodak commercials have garnered thirty-six international awards for Thompson, and he has also written on Ford, Lever Brothers, and other accounts. Mr. Thoren holds a 1951 summa cum laude B.A. in Journalism from Notre Dame, and worked his way to Thompson as a writer and TV commercial producer through four other advertising agencies.

Mr. Thoren is married with four children and commutes to New York daily from his home in Connecticut. As Granger Tripp indicates, he had a "continuing assignment" to think up picture-taking television commercials for the Kodak account. As with any commuter, this provokes a lot of day-dreaming on the train. In this discussion, supplemented by his original word-for-word draft script (see Appendix B), Mr. Thoren details the birth of the "Yesterdays" idea and his part in all the events that followed thereon:

I went back through my files — and came up with "the beginning" of "Yesterdays": four little pieces of yellow paper, the original script, dated April 15, 1966. I read it carefully. I had forgotten how well the original concept had been executed. I think a TV writer is happiest when the idea he has conceived travels through all the complexities of production without being changed, mangled or destroyed. Read the original and as-aired scripts — and I think you'll understand why I was so totally satisfied with the way Warren and Mike shepherded the idea through to completion.

People often ask how I get my ideas for Kodak scripts. When I think about it — which isn't too often — I realize there's a different creative road leading to each and every script. Take "Yesterdays," for instance.

Peg and Harry Mann were two *actual* people; they lived next door to me at the time the script was written. They were a childless couple who had been married for over twenty-five years and their devotion to one another was extremely strong. They were also the picture-takingest people I had ever known. Pictures were everywhere in their house; in frames on tables, on the walls, in albums and scattered in a million places.

As these facts jelled in my mind, I thought they could be the basis for a commercial. I tried working up a plot for them — but couldn't make any headway until I realized I *had* to give them children. So I "borrowed" Clay Hallock (who lived on the other side of the Manns) and Holt Ardry (who lived across the street from them). I gave these two "sons" to the Manns — and *presto*, the plot took shape!

We'd discover the Manns in their basement, trying to clean it up. Peg would find an old carton stuffed with pictures and memorabilia. At the same time, Harry would discover a pile of records, pick out an old favorite, and play it on an ancient wind-up phonograph. Then, by combining audio and video, we'd be able to relive the Manns' life together. Twenty-five years in two minutes — not bad, if it worked!

The development of the video idea went smoothly enough, but I still hadn't decided on the record. Then one night, completely by accident, I was watching a variety show on television. I heard Jimmy Durante sing the beautiful Jerome Kern-Otto Harbach classic, "Yesterdays." *Click*: the perfect song for a perfect audio-video marriage!

As Granger said, this script was not written for any specific assignment. Kodak's so-called motivational commercial assignment was an open-end one. Whenever an idea struck, Granger would look at a script. I can't actually remember exactly how long it took me to write the script in my head, but I think I mulled over the idea for at least a month before hitting the typewriter. Once I started typing, it practically wrote itself.

Granger liked the script and passed it to the Kodak client, Ted Genock, without any changes. Ted also liked it and gave approval for its production.

Warren Aldoretta was assigned as producer. He and I talked at great length before he started talking to production companies.

The production job was finally awarded to MPO, with Mike Cimino as director.

Mike, Warren and I got together for a pre-pre-production meeting. We pulled the commercial apart, chewed over every nuance — and in all honesty, had a few constructive battles.

Mike, for instance, was adamantly opposed to using the "Yesterdays" song.* He felt it much too sentimental. He felt the video would be strong enough without it. On the other hand, I felt it had validity; it came from the time of the Manns' courtship and was a favorite, recognizable standard with a broad portion of our audience. Mike wasn't too happy, but he let me win that round.

*Mike appears to remember this disagreement "through a fog-filter." See p. 71 — *Ed.*

I lost a few others, however. I conceived the setting in a cellar. I felt the low ceiling and tight quarters would enhance the commercial's intimacy. Mike and Warren, however, made a strong plea for an attic. They felt such an attic setting would offer better angles, better sources of light and better room for shooting. Looking back now, I must admit a writer can often have blinders on. One of the reasons I fought for the cellar was because the Manns actually lived in a ranch house that didn't have an attic! Mike and Warren finally convinced me (and in the end, I was glad they did) that the attic was best.

Another point of difference was whether the grandchild should be a boy or a girl. The original script called for a girl. Mike wanted a boy. I couldn't see how it made a particle of difference — so I went along with him.

But I disagreed about the singer. I felt strongly that the song should be sung by a male vocalist. The Thirties — when the song first came out — was the time of singers like Russ Columbo, Bing Crosby, Rudy Vallee and Dick Powell; the day of the male vocalist.

By the time a final decision to go with a female vocalist was made, however, I was actually quite far removed from the spot. After that meeting with Mike and Warren, I received an assignment to produce another Kodak script I had written, in California. By the time I got back, all the stills had been shot and the live shoot was scheduled. I looked at the stills and thought they were fantastic, so I strolled over to MPO to watch the live shooting for half-an-hour or so. Karl Hueglin's set was incredible. And what Mike was doing with the two actors was beautiful. I hate unnecessary people hanging around my sets, so I had a few words with Warren (who was so excited about what was happening that by this time he was practically hanging from the lighting grid) and left.

Again because of other assignments, I didn't re-enter the scene until the track was being completed. Not happy with the selection of a female vocalist, I was even unhappier at the idea of the stuck record; I didn't feel such a gimmick was necessary. There was an esthetic purity and honesty to the film. The track, I feel, is slightly false, mechanical, overproduced. I realize these are merely subjective criticisms; on the whole, the commercial turned out beautifully. To see one of your ideas come to life so close to what you have originally conceived is a real kick. One of the biggest!

THE CREATIVE DIRECTOR

Once the ideas for "Yesterdays" had been approved internally at J. Walter Thompson, they were presented to Eastman Kodak for comment, possible revision, and eventually for a production go-ahead. Granger Tripp details that procedure:

Once a commercial has been written, it has a long and difficult row to hoe, before it can find its way to the television screen. The agency and group that can protect the integrity of an idea and deliver it intact to the home screen will be blessed with great success.

Let me tell you briefly what happened with "Yesterdays," and then go a little deeper into the subject of commercial presentation as a whole — because this commercial was an exception.

You have heard it said in earlier discussions that Kodak is an unusual client in many respects. One of them is the professionalism of their people, with whom we deal. Kodak's Broadcast Advertising Manager, Ted Genock, began his career as a recording engineer, then became a newsreel cameraman, and then a newsreel supervisor. For a while, he was manager of Tele-News in New York. Ted Genock is a thorough technician; he understands every aspect of our business better than we do.

His assistant, John Stott, was manager of a film lab, and understands the operation of a lab optical house better than we do. So we don't feel the necessity of explaining the technical aspects of television as much with them as we do with other Thompson clients.

The presentation of "Yesterdays" was very simple. We put it in an envelope and sent it up to Rochester. They said, "O.K. Go ahead."

I wish the advertising business always worked like that. It doesn't. It doesn't always happen like that on Kodak, either. But this was part of a continuing assignment, and, because Kodak's taste and judgment are excellent, they were able to recognize a good commercial when they saw it.

Only after "Yesterdays" was approved, did we have a storyboard made. Hal Taylor was in charge of that operation for us. His storyboards follow the original script quite closely and as you see, the finished production is quite close to the boards. It shows Hal did a very good job capturing the spirit Ken put into the script.

THE ART DIRECTOR

Hal Taylor is a Senior Art Director with J. Walter Thompson Co. His first job in art direction was with a local Pittsburgh department store; his first advertising agency position was with William Esty in New York. He was soon deep in TV commercial work; "Klondike Pete," one of Mr. Taylor's Ballantine Ale Spots (produced in the 1950's with Joop Gesink's puppets in Holland) already sits securely in The Classic Commercial Hall of Fame.

After a spell at Benton & Bowles, Mr. Taylor moved to Thompson; he has been there nine years. At Thompson, he is responsible for visualization of advertising ideas in all media, for a group of clients that includes Kodak. Storyboard procedure on "Yesterdays," while normal for Kodak commercials, did not reflect standard U.S. agency practice. The points of departure, however, throw the function of storyboards in different advertising situations into sharp relief:

Granger has told you the various ways in which a storyboard can be made. Before we get to the "Yesterdays" storyboard, I would like to point out the reason for *any* storyboard. *Storyboards are for clients*; they serve to visualize a script. A television commercial *script* — its left hand side devoted to *video*, its right hand side to *audio* — is a typed description of the action. Not a tape, it literally has no sound; not a series of pictures, it has no true video. It is only a more or less detailed account of what will take place in the commercial as certain words are spoken.

But a script is clumsy. You can read across the page — first the video, to visualize the action; then the audio, to get the corresponding words. Or you can read down the video side, then down the audio. Any way you look at it, it's clumsy, and hard to visualize.

Storyboards grew out of a genuine need to help a client visualize the commercial easily and quickly. Most clients were accustomed to layouts of print advertising with all the elements placed neatly in position. Imagine presenting a client with a script — instead of a layout — for a print ad! The script would have to include a lengthy description of the main art or photo with a notation that it would occupy a certain amount of space, plus a description of the secondary illustration which would depict such-and-such, then a headline and what type it would be set in, then the body copy and what that would be set in, and finally a notation about where the corporate signature would go. Obviously, a print *layout* is much simpler and easier for the client to visualize.

The television storyboard serves the client in the same way — even the most visually-minded clients (into which category Kodak certainly falls).

To perform its proper function as an implementation of the script, a storyboard should preserve a rough, sketchy feeling. It should not be carried too far. It should interpret the *visual* intent of the commercial, *but not make a visual commitment.* I even prefer storyboards to be sketched in black-and-white, so there is no commitment as to color of clothing or furnishings. (Also black-and-white boards photostat better than color boards.)

The rough storyboard is also valuable to the production house; its very sketchiness suggests the total concept of the commercial. An "overly-conceived" board goes beyond its reason for being; it attempts to live a life of its own. Sometimes a producer may feel he wants his storyboard to exude a particular cinematic quality. It can't be done. One cannot convey cinematic quality in a storyboard. What usually happens is that the storyboard ends up too well delineated, and still does not have the feeling of film. It is not a film; nothing an artist does to it will ever make it so. It is only a script with illustrations. It has to be accepted as such.

After all this talk about the value of rough storyboards, how did the board for "Yesterdays" turn out to be so buttoned-up? For one thing, notice the date: "September 29th." If you remember, Ken Thoren wrote his first draft on April 15th, five and one-half months earlier.

Working with just Ken's script, there were many pre-production meetings before September. The "Yesterdays" storyboard was created to reflect all the thinking that came out of those meetings. By the time it was made, we felt it could be detailed enough to have the flavor and mood of what we were aiming for in the production.

But even here, a rough storyboard was made first. I sketched the rough, then turned it over to one of Thompson's illustrators, Everett Hibbard. Hib loved the idea of this commercial; he brought a wealth of detail and feeling into these finished sketches. Generally speaking, this type of "mood" storyboard is difficult to achieve, almost impossible to get in a rough rendition. For many clients and production companies, a *specific* storyboard such as this for "Yesterdays" may be too much of a commitment. It may be too tight; the producer may feel he cannot swing with it. But in the case of "Yesterdays," it represented the thinking of all the people concerned with its production: the writer, the producer, the director, and everyone else. That's why it worked.

EASTMAN KODAK TV COMMERCIAL
DISNEY   11/19/67
PT STILL: "YESTERDAYS"
TWO MINUTES - COLOR FILM T 7025
CL. APP. 8/11/66
SB. SEPTEMBER 29, 1966

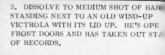

1. FADE UP ON DOLLY SHOT MOVING TO-
WARDS ATTIC WINDOW FROM THE OUTSIDE.
SUPER: "KODAK"

2. CROSS DISSOLVE TO INTERIOR OF ATTIC
AND CONTINUE TO DOLLY. WE SEE A
CLUTTERED AND YET NOT DISREPUTABLE
LOOKING COLLECTION OF PROPS ANY FAMI-
LY MIGHT COLLECT OVER THE YEARS: TOYS,
A CRIB FILLED WITH BOXES, CHRISTMAS
DECORATIONS, A FEW PIECES OF OLD
FURNITURE, ETC.

3. DISSOLVE TO MEDIUM SHOT OF HAR
STANDING NEXT TO AN OLD WIND-UP
VICTROLA WITH ITS LID UP. HE'S OPE
FRONT DOORS AND HAS TAKEN OUT STA
OF RECORDS.

SFX: OUTDOORS SOUNDS: I.E., BIRDS, KIDS
PLAYING DOWN THE STREET, LAWN
MOWER.

SOUNDS: (WE HEAR PEG AND HARRY TALK-
ING TO EACH OTHER BUT THEIR VOICES ARE
SO LOW, IT'S ALMOST AS IF WE WERE
EVESDROPPING. THEIR REMARKS ARE AD
LIB.)

8. CUT TO TIGHT SHOT OF CARTON. LIKE
MOST PEOPLE -- THE MANNS NEVER WERE
"ALBUM-KEEPERS". FOR YEARS THEY
MERELY STUFFED ALL THEIR SNAPSHOTS
INTO THE TOP DRAWER OF THE DINING ROOM
CHEST. WHEN THAT BEGAN TO OVERFLOW,
THEY PUT ALL THEIR PICTURES INTO THIS
TRUNK. WE SEE IT'S HAPHAZARDLY STUF-
FED WITH NOT ONLY PICTURES BUT ALSO
OLD NEWSPAPERS, PROGRAMS, MENUS, ETC.

7. CUT TO PEG AS SHE LIFTS OUT TOP
COMPARTMENT.

9. CUT TO WIDER SHOT OF PEG AS SH
CARTON ON LAP. SHE SITS IN MOTHY
STUFFED CHAIR AND ASKS HARRY TO
HER.

STORYBOARD

DISSOLVE TO CLOSE SHOT OF PEG AS
HE PICKS UP A TATTERED OLD TEDDY
EAR. SHE LOOKS AT IT REMEMBERING
HE DAYS HOLT -- OR WAS IT CLAY? --
ARRIED IT EVERYWHERE.

5. DISSOLVE TO LONG SHOT AS PEG OPENS
TRUNK.

6. CUT TO SHOT OF HARRY LOOKING RE-
FLECTIVELY AT A RECORD. HE WINDS
UP VICTROLA AND STARTS TO PUT RECORD
ON TURNTABLE.

0. CUT TO TIGHT SHOT OF HARRY PUTTING
EEDLE ON RECORD.

11. PULL BACK AS HE GOES TO JOIN PEG

12. CUT TO MEDIUM SHOT OF PEG AND
HARRY LOOKING AT SNAPSHOTS.

MUSIC: THE RECORD STARTS. THE SONG IS
"YESTERDAY". (WE EITHER SIMULATE THE
ARRANGEMENT AND THE SOUND OF A 30'S
SINGER OR WE SEARCH FOR AN ACTUAL
RECORDING OF THE SONG OF THAT TIME.)

SINGERS:
Yesterdays, yesterday...

13. CUT TO SNAPSHOT: PEG AND HARRY IN THEIR EARLY TWENTIES IN BRAND NEW CAR. PEG SITS IN RUMBLE SEAT SMILING AT CAMERA.

14. CUT TO SNAPSHOT: PEG AND HARRY ON A PICNIC. (NATURALLY, THESE ARE ONLY SUGGESTED SHOTS. THE REAL THING OR ACTUAL PICTURES WOULD BE USED.)

15. CUT TO TWO SHOT OF HARRY AND P ENJOYING THEIR PICTURES.

Days I knew as happy...

sweet sequester'd days.

Olden days,

19. CUT TO SNAPSHOT: PEG AND HARRY WITH HOLT, THEIR FIRST BORN.

20. CUT TO SNAPSHOT: PEG WITH TWO YEAR-OLD HOLT AND CLAY, AN INFANT IN HER ARMS.

21. CUT TO SNAPSHOT: FAMILY ALL T GETHER. BOYS A LITTLE OLDER AND I IN ARMY UNIFORM.

Then gay youth was mine,

Truth was mine.

Joyous, free...

CUT TO SNAPSHOT: WEDDING POSE.

17. CUT TO SNAPSHOT: HONEYMOON SHOT.

18. CUT TO SNAPSHOT: CU OF PEG.

Golden days,

Days of mad romance...

and love.

22. CUT TO SNAPSHOT: BOYS WITH HARRY THEY'RE STILL A LITTLE OLDER. HE'S BACK IN CIVVIES AGAIN.

23. CUT TO SNAPSHOT: HARRY AND PEG STAND WITH HOLT IN HIS COLLEGE CAP AND GOWN.

...and flaming life...

...forsooth, was mine.

24. CUT TO TIGHT SHOT OF PEG STILL
LOOKING AT PICTURES. HER FACE RE-
FLECTS A POIGNANT FEELING BUT THEN...

25. BREAKS INTO AN OPEN LAUGH AS
CAMERA PULLS BACK TO INCLUDE HARRY
IN SHOT WHO'S SHOWING PEG A SHOT HE
HAS FOUND.

26. HOLD AS PEG AND HARRY EXCHANGE
LOVING LOOKS.

Sad am I...

Glad am I...

For today I'm dreaming of yesterdays.

30. CUT TO SHOT OF CAMERA AND FILM
SITTING ON FRONT STOOP.

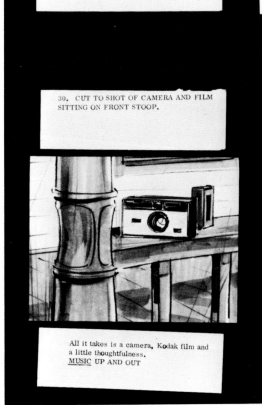

All it takes is a camera, Kodak film and
a little thoughtfulness.
<u>MUSIC</u> UP AND OUT

27. THEIR SPELL IS BROKEN AT SOUND OF CAR HORN. BOTH LOOK OFF SCREEN AND QUICKLY GET UP AND LEAVE.

28. DISSOLVE TO FRONT PORCH AS HARRY AND PEG HURRY OUT TO GREET HOLT, HIS WIFE AND THEIR LITTLE GIRL WHO HAS JUST DRIVEN OVER FOR A VISIT.

29. DISSOLVE TO SHOT OF HARRY TAKING A PICTURE OF GRANDAUGHTER WITH KODAK INSTAMATIC 104.

SFX: CAR HORN BLOWS OUTSIDE
MUSIC: SEGUE TO MODERN, UNDER-SCORING ARRANGEMENT OF "YESTER-DAYS".

SFX: AS BEFORE, WE HEAR AD LIB REMARKS UNDER THE MUSIC -- AS IF WE WERE BYSTANDERS AT SCENE.

ANNOUNCER: (VO)
Yesterday ... today ... and tomorrow are yours to keep--in pictures.

THE CREATIVE DIRECTOR

Granger Tripp resumes his discussion of the problems involved
in making a creative presentation to the Client:

The storyboard was not a wasted exercise, even though the commercial had
already been approved. It was used in many discussions among Warren
Aldoretta, Mike Cimino and everyone else involved in the production.

A storyboard is important because it helps avoid possible misunderstandings. Two people can read the same paragraph, and no matter how
clear the writer may think that paragraph is, it is always possible for misunderstandings to occur.

As I said, the presentation and approval of "Yesterdays" were simple;
not typical of what happens in the advertising business.

I would like to run through some other ways agencies present their
commercials to clients, and some of the advantages and disadvantages of
each. It runs the whole gamut.

I think the ideal solution would be to call up your client on the telephone, or talk to him over lunch, and say, "We have an idea and this is
what we want to do," and he would say, "Yes, go ahead." That would be
the minimum possible approval procedure. Obviously it leaves a great deal
of room for misunderstanding, so that procedure isn't often used.

What does happen sometimes is that we present a written synopsis of
an idea *without* a script. This is a useful method, if you are sending production people out to get broad coverage of an area of activity, or to do a
documentary style of commercial

Next step up this scale in the degree of finish in what you present,
would be a *shooting script*, which is what we did in the case of "Yesterdays."
This method is inexpensive, quick, and convenient. If you have a client
who is well-trained, it is a useful way to obtain his approval. Again it is
possible, with the best of intentions on both sides, for misunderstandings to
arise. What seems perfectly clear to the writer, the group head and the
account people may seem perfectly clear to the client too, but his understanding may be entirely different.

A friend of mine used to say, "Think how many people *push,* when
the door says 'Pull.' " It is impossible to avoid the possibility of misunderstanding.

Next step up the scale is the *storyboard*. This is perhaps the most-used
method of client presentation. It can be very elaborate, very rough, or very

simple. It can be what we call a "concept board," which is a single picture (or perhaps a group of pictures) that attempt to convey the mood or atmosphere of the commercial, without attempting to do what Hal Taylor and his group eventually did in this case — drawing each frame and relating it specifically to the audio.

Well, storyboards, too, have their drawbacks. One is that we now get into the area where we may get pinned down. The board may be so finished that the client will say, "Yes, that's exactly what I want," and Ray Fragasso and his production crew have been left no room for maneuver. Our standing instruction to Ray and his people is, "Come *back* with a better commercial than you went *out* with!"

We want them to improve on the storyboard they start with. We try not to pin them down to a literal interpretation of the board. In this particular case, they stuck pretty much to the original board, but we still want to maintain as much freedom for them as we can.

Another problem with storyboards is this: It's hard to lead your audience through a storyboard without having them become distracted by a particular frame, that may be relatively unimportant in the total commercial. You can't say to them, "Look, the motion represented by this frame is going to be on for five seconds; while this one is on for twenty seconds." It's hard to lead them through a board at the proper pace; a commercial, after all, is movement. It never stands still like an ad. So the time factor is a problem.

The next step up the scale of complication is a big one. We can put storyboards on slides, and turn out the lights. I always feel this is a dangerous step, because as soon as you put people in a darkened room, and put something on the screen, they automatically compare what they see with other commercials with which they are familiar. You put it up on a screen and they say, "God, that's not as good as the commercial I saw last night." Well, of course it isn't, because it's a series of slides and the soundtrack is not finished; it's a rough presentation.

So you run a risk when you put the storyboard frames on slides and turn out the lights. You are inviting people to compare what you show them with finished commercials. But it *does* allow you to control the *time*. You can sit there with your projector, and leave one frame on the screen longer than others.

The next step up the scale — it's becoming fairly popular — is *cineboards*. You take storyboard frames like these, deliver them to an "animation stand" house, and have them put it all on 16mm film for you, at a relatively modest price. You provide them with a finished soundtrack.

Again, this looks like a finished commercial. It's an advantage, because it helps the client see almost exactly what he's going to get. It's a danger, because you pin yourself down to what was on the storyboard. You may eliminate creativity that your production company could supply.

Another thing tried nowadays is "Super-8" film. It is very useful, very instructive I think, for people to take Super-8 cameras out and use them to experiment and try their own ideas. We have had considerable success with it. Warren Aldoretta did a very interesting 8mm film in Central Park which Ray later converted into a commercial, for last year's Academy Awards show.

That was useful, because it let us all see the spirit that Warren had in mind for the commercial. Super-8 film is inexpensive, anybody can use the camera, and with a little effort, you can edit it down into a rough idea of what the commercial might be. This is useful and instructive, although again it may pin you down.

Next step up the scale — and almost the last one — is the experimental "test" film. If you cannot convince a client any other way, you can go out and spend quite a little money to get a small film company to make you a 16mm commercial that will represent the idea you have in mind. Again this may limit what you can do in the finished commercial. And again it invites direct comparison with a finished commercial, which may be dangerous.

The last and ultimate step, which very few agencies I know of undertake, is to go out and shoot the commercial itself. That's when you are really desperate; you gamble with your own money. It has been done. An agency will go out and shoot a finished commercial, show it to the client, and say, "Here it is, this is what we want to run." If he accepts it, you get your money back. If he doesn't, you don't get your money back. Obviously that is not practiced very often.

Now, to get back to "Yesterdays." We have an approved storyboard or shooting script. What do we do with it? In our group we turn it over to Ray Fragasso, who by now has already been intimately involved in the creation of the commercial. He has had much to say about the concept, about every aspect of it. It's important that he be involved before it is presented or sold to the client, for he may point out some aspects we have overlooked. It adds a great deal to any commercial creation to have both the art director and the production head involved at the earliest possible stage.

Thus it's no surprise to Ray when we come to him and say, "This commercial has been approved. It's now ready to be produced, and we'd like the answer print at a certain time, if possible."

THE PRODUCTION GROUP HEAD

Raymond Fragasso is Production Group Head on Kodak at J. Walter Thompson. A native New Yorker, he studied civil engineering at City College before entering the advertising field in 1953. After five years at the Kudner Agency, he moved to Lennen & Newell, and in 1960, joined Thompson as a TV commercial producer. Since then, his responsibilities have expanded to a number of important Agency accounts.

With Ken Thoren's creative work approved for production by Kodak, it was passed to Matt Harlib, Ray's boss. Then Mr. Fragasso — with his producer Warren Aldoretta — began the very practical process of deciding how to get what was wanted onto the TV screen.

At this stage, differences of creative opinion were abundant. Slowly, unworkable directions were eliminated and the joint idea the entire group eventually underwrote began to take shape. Ray Fragasso discusses his part in this development of "Yesterdays":

To learn everyone seems to value my opinion comes as a complete surprise; if they had listened to my opinions on the making of "Yesterdays," it would have been a complete abortion.

To start, when Ken first showed me his script draft on the commuter train one night, I said, "Well, Ken, it's beautiful, lovely, sentimental; but it goes exactly against everything we've been saying: 'Save those precious moments, remember those beautiful memories, save them in pictures.' Here you've got them thrown in a box in the cellar; it goes against everything we've been advertising."

In spite of that, Ken went ahead, and eventually got client approval for production. When Warren was assigned and we all were discussing production approaches, Ken seemed absolutely right in thinking we'd never be able to duplicate the necessary photographs. "We have to find a couple who has their own photographs," I agreed. Again I was wrong.

The third time I was off base was when they showed me the rough-cut. I said, "Well, you've done a terrific job of moving me, up in the attic, but with all that contemporary music, you've lost me." Anyhow, things were changed around a bit, and so were my opinions.

I was handed the initial idea and started thinking about production. I wondered which producer would best qualify for this particular concept. We have a very well-rounded group of producers; all kinds — writer/producers, art director/producers, and producer/producers, and I think our Group has the best of the lot at Thompson.

Picking the right producer for a concept is only part of the job. The other consideration with Kodak is always to be ahead of the times. They are indeed a sophisticated client and know what good film production is all about, so we are always trying to find "tomorrow's look." (Even while we are here paying tribute to "Yesterdays," we are really thinking about next year's Academy Awards program.)

In the area of style in selecting a production company, it is no great task to pick a major company on the basis of sheer professionalism, because: (1) we expect professionalism; (2) we pay for professionalism; (3) we better get it for the kind of money we are paying! What we *do* look for in this selection is the kind of director to whom we can give an awful lot of freedom in execution, to see what he brings back in subtlety and nuance. It is hard to define, but you know it when you see it, like the subtlety and touches Mike Cimino and everyone else put into such small details as the photographs, where not a hair was out of place. So we look for the nuances a director can bring to a given concept. We also look ahead to new styles and new techniques, perhaps from outside "normal" commercial production areas.

Something I have read recently explains all of our thinking in producing commercials for Kodak:

"Anyone who seeks the security of the familiar will bring about his own obsolescence in the world of tomorrow." That's how we like to approach TV production in our Group.

NOTE: The questions and discussion that followed this presentation appear on p. 145 ff.

7
Market
Planning

THE TV FESTIVAL MANAGER

Now we reach the source where it all began — Kodak's marketing needs. There is so much interplay in this discussion; just as the Agency's creative team reflected a very positive view of the Account, now does the Account give high praise to the Agency's creative effort. But behind that surface praise lies a subtler kind of appreciation that says, "You really understood what we needed, you gave it to us easily, and it was successful." Again, a credit to teamwork.

How does one measure the "success" of "Yesterdays"? Hardly by shelf inventories or factory shipments of Kodak Film and Instamatic 104's; as Alan Anderson pointed out, "Yesterdays" was only one of 87 Kodak spots used on air in 1967. By letters of praise Ted Genock received? Or by the knowledge that everyone who sees "Yesterdays" seems moved by it? Perhaps the reactions of audiences at TV commercial festivals around the world offer a sounder clue.

Wallace A. Ross is Founder and Managing Director of the American Television Commercials Festival. He is a graduate of Cornell University, and served as a Lieutenant in World War II. After discharge, he started an early newsletter on the television industry, and then became an executive with the New York Film Producers Association.

In 1960, wishing to upgrade the public image and quality of American television commercials, Mr. Ross launched his

Festival — which (with the present Editor as its quondam producer) has since become a successful international institution, attracting commercial entries from all over the world.

Here Mr. Ross provides an evaluation of public reaction to "Yesterdays" at mass screenings both in this country and overseas:

The validity of awards for TV advertising still remains to be measured. There are a lot of award functions. I would not vouch for all of them. They are all well meant. As with anything planned in the awards area, there is at least some hope of doing something constructive, but not all functions are operated (or judged) well. The fact that "Yesterdays" has won thirteen awards around the world impresses but does not overwhelm me.

Let me tell you briefly how "Yesterdays" did with the advertising professionals who judged the American TV Commercial Festival last year. We organize entries on a product category basis; it's an attempt to appraise advertising as opposed to technique.

In today's sophisticated production world, we take technique for granted. Exceptional, that's something else, but we *assume* "good technique." In essence, our judges are looking for concepts and ideas.

We don't give them any "success story." We don't give them the background. We organize a group of related commercials, so judges have a frame of reference. They can see how others do the same thing. Over the years Kodak and Polaroid have vied in our "Gift Item" category. It's a hard-fought competition; Polaroid does brilliant work. Kodak has held a little edge down through the years and has won our top award in that category a bit more often.

They offer two diametrically different approaches. I think the people at Thompson and Kodak recognize this; they are not selling in as sophisticated a fashion or to as sophisticated a market. After all, Polaroid has been a more expensive product, until very recently.

There have been Polaroid winners — there have been Kodak winners. For the past few years, it has been pretty much Kodak.

In the Festival, where annually we assess about 2,500 U.S. TV commercials, we judge preliminarily with "excellent, very good, good, fair, poor" — five choices. Tabulators then assign a 5, 4, 3, 2, 1, numerical value to each of those votes. A perfect score would be 5; the average is a 3.5.

"Yesterdays" scored 4.5 in the preliminaries. That's about as high as you're going to get. 4.5 is pretty good. It means almost everybody said, "This is an excellent commercial." And the judges were all advertising professionals.

On the other hand, one Polaroid had a 4.0 — that was next highest. So here is this ding-dong battle of communicating a similar type of product. Another Kodak commercial, "Summer Place" had a 3.8; but the highest score, 4.5, went to "Yesterdays."

In the finals, we pull up three or four out of each category. This particular category is always excellently produced, excellent conceived. It involves not only cameras, but pens and other recreational gift items and personal items — shavers, personal appliances, things like that. All well done, all able to be demonstrated, all very competitive.

The finals are based on a different score value. We knock off fair and poor. We assume if they got to the finals, they are "good, very good, exceptional." We go on a basis of 1 for good; 4 for very good; 8 for exceptional. Don't ask me how we got to that, but that's it — 8, 4, 1; a perfect score would be 8.

Kodak won its category with a 6.5 — not the highest of all the categories. For example, in the bath soap and deodorant category, Ban's deodorant campaign took a 6.8. In the pharmaceutical/analgesic category, Excedrin's "Tax Audit" (which was also voted the "best overall campaign") took a 6.9. Also in that category, the Alka-Seltzer "Stomach Talk" had a 6.6. In the cereal food category, Kellogg's had a 6.8. The highest rated commercial for the year was 7.1, for the Union Carbide campaign.

So "Yesterdays' " 6.5 was not the highest score, but more than respectable — between "very good" and "exceptional."

Now I have a more astonishing story to tell — and I am happy to tell it. In terms of audience reaction, particularly with large groups of people, it is fascinating what, down through the years, Kodak has been able to accomplish. There is a distinct emotional relationship between their commercials and a large audience viewing them.

Of course television is directed to and seen by either one person or a small family group. You don't have that infectious reaction you get out of a large audience. Frankly, people who produce commercials for the cinema try for that spreading reaction.

And most of my screenings after the Festival *are* for large groups — 200, 400, 1,500 people — advertising people in some instances, students at colleges, civic groups, Rotary and the like. For the last six months of every year, I travel — that's all I do. I get on a plane and show the reel, around the country and around the world.

I would say that of all the commercials on last year's reel of winners, "Yesterdays" was the best received by large groups of people. What makes me say that? Applause. Can you imagine people sitting there, literally *applauding*! There are yocks of laughter at the "Ban," because it hits you over the head; there is appreciation of the Alka-Seltzer "Stomach Talk"; at what Union Carbide was able to do; and laughter at the Kellogg commercial that scored so high. But the only one that got sustained, continued applause, everywhere I went, was this Kodak commercial "Yesterdays."

I might also say the same thing applied to "Sunrise-Sunset," the year before. It also applied to the first of the Kodak spots in this genre, "Turn Around," the pictorial history of a young girl growing up — in stills by her father — combined beautifully into a 90-second commercial to a ballad, some years ago.

So emotional contact was established, and I would guess this is the A-1, prime goal "Yesterdays" tries to achieve, along with other Kodak advertising. Whether it was in Germany, Japan or Italy — it was universal — the minimum dialogue involved helped make it universal.

Can I tell you how many times I've seen "Yesterdays"? Three or four hundred times at least. I still don't see it without it grabbing me just a little bit. I understand that at the Academy Awards, where Kodak is the sponsor, the blasé and sophisticated audience gave it sustained applause that very few other Award announcements received.

I add this testimony to the effectiveness of the communication. I don't know a thing about the sales. I do know the audience reaction.

THE BUSINESS MANAGER

Alfred R. Tennyson has been with J. Walter Thompson Co. for four years, currently as Commercial Production Administrator and Business Manager. He attended Yale University. Mr. Tennyson, previously a band leader, song writer, theatre director and night manager of a New York City radio station, moved into broadcast advertising at Newell Emmett and Kenyon & Eckhardt in the 1950's.

It is Mr. Tennyson's job at Thompson to see that the Production Department operates in a businesslike manner. Here he underlines the importance of holding to a "business" concept in broadcast advertising:

It seems appropriate here to make the point that advertising is a *business* — a creative business for sure, but very definitely a business. "Yesterdays" has a business record, as well as the creative record we've already heard about.

The commercial started off as all our commercials do — with a number, to identify this particular project and follow it through its complete history.

One of the first official documents to set the commercial in motion was an approved formal estimate. This was the result of all the calculations and anticipated charges, turned over to the client for his official approval.

That's the pricing we establish for ourselves. Everything past that point has to live up to the estimate.

On it we show, in addition to the cost of producing the commercial, an estimate of any outside art work that might be involved. Talent is also a separate cost, as is music. Once the estimate is approved, the project has its official "go-ahead."

From that point, the basic production agreement itself is handled by a simplified five-page contract. In addition to being the official document — the agreement between the film company and J. Walter Thompson on behalf of our client — two pages become purchase orders, so that at the time bills are sent in, a page of the initial contract identifies and verifies the bill to speed processing. One copy is retained in our bookkeeping section, to anticipate charges that come in later, so we're not surprised with the bills.

Everything other than the production agreement with the film company is handled by purchase orders. We have four copies to our purchase order. One is retained at the agency to anticipate charges. Another is retained by the producer. The supplier receives two copies. One is for his file and one must be sent in with his bill, again identified and anticipated right from the beginning.

Our agreement with talent, of course, is the Screen Actor's Guild contract, and we have forms for those items. The musicians have their own AFM contract.

Once the commercial is produced, the initial assignment is complete. Printing of additional prints to use on programs and so forth is covered in another budget.

The film elements themselves are put in a vault. All the business material is retained in a little folder that identifies the project by name and by number, and is maintained in our files for years for auditing purposes. It came in handy for this Workshop, by the way; we were able to dig back and find out many of the details we've discussed.

To further emphasize the fact that this is a business, I was impressed with the information different participants were still able to come up with. Casting reported there were twelve people they hoped to see in connection with the commercial who were not available, because they were out of town or working elsewhere; an indication of the records our casting people keep.

The fact that sound tracks were available to us two-and-a-half years after the fact; the fact that the work print is still in pretty good shape; the fact that our fashion lady was able to tell us she used sixteen sources to rent costumes for "Yesterdays" — all indicate that underneath this creativity is an urgent framework that permits us to finish on time, and at the agreed-upon price. A very definite structure is an awfully important part of what we do. *In fact and necessity, advertising is first of all a business.*

THE MANAGEMENT SUPERVISOR

Wyatte Hicks, Management Supervisor at J. Walter Thompson Co., bears the agency responsibility for close, top-level relationship with the Agency's client, Eastman Kodak. He puts the final stamp of approval on all the marketing formulations Thompson prepares for Kodak, discusses them with the Client, and then re-transmits them to his own creative people for execution.

Mr. Hicks has served Thompson in account management for almost ten years. Hailing from Arkansas, he received his Journalism B.A. from the University of Missouri in 1943 at the ripe old age of 18. Since then — with time out for the Army — Mr. Hicks has worked "on the account side" for four major advertising agencies, in and out of New York City.

Here he discusses the general functions of an account representative, and the particular nature of his work on the Kodak account:

Let me establish for you the role the account man played in this operation. Whether you call him an account representative, an account supervisor, a management supervisor or account executive — we go by many names, some publishable, some not — we all perform basically the same role.

We represent the agency's total services and capabilities and potential performance record to a client. By the same token, we have to return from the client — and represent his interests within the agency. This is a bit of a dichotomy; it does tend to split you up a bit. You often have divided loyalties, because (strangely enough?) your client and your agency people don't always agree. And you find you're right in the middle.

This requires that the account man, more than anything else, have a complete understanding of the client's business, what his needs are, what he's up to, what he's trying to achieve; and at the same time recognize the requirements, if you will, of the creative procedure, the research procedure, the media procedure, and the television procedure — and all the other services within the agency that have to be brought together to produce a final result that will pay off for our client.

This means the account man does two things generally — planning and execution. The planning is important, so he is somewhat more identifiable in the planning process than in the execution. Planning is the establishment of strategy. *What* should a client do? How should he do it? How much money should he invest? These are some of the things that put together an advertising campaign. Once the campaign is approved, then execution largely falls on the shoulders of other people.

The account man may still feel some responsibility for it; he may still feel he ought to supervise or look over a shoulder now and then — but basically he now has turned the job over to experts who execute specific functions — specialists — since no one wants to be called an "expert." You use specialists to help in the planning phases, too. You use research specialists to find out all the facts about the market place, media specialists who establish whether you should be doing thirty-second commercials, or print advertising in magazines, or posting car cards in the subway. You utilize them in the planning stage, and others in the execution stages.

The account representative has to energize the team, to worry about the timetable and the budgets — not only the portion already referred to for commercial production — but the *total* budget, along with media costs and other costs. And of course he has to worry about such small things as client schedules; when they want to see the progress of work, when it has to be produced and finally placed on the air.

To get down to the specifics of this commercial — how the account representative functioned in this area — let us presume he established with the client an understanding, an agreement on the strategy involved. The basic strategy here is simple — make people want to take pictures. Make people value having a record of memories, happy events, and other occasions in their lives. A nice gentle objective — but it's good and bad. It's *good* because it leaves a great deal of freedom for creation, for executing the message of making people want to take pictures. It may be *bad,* because it isn't terribly specific.

For instance, our plans for "Yesterdays" didn't say; "We want to reach people of a certain age, of a certain demographic quality — people who live in a certain area, people who have so much education, have a certain income." Those are the type of facts we try to draw out, every time we put an advertising message in front of the public. Obviously, we like to know as much as possible about the man or woman we are talking to. We can then be more specific and effective with our message.

In the case of "Yesterdays" we were only concerned with wanting people to want pictures. How do we do it, with this emotional tug Wally Ross mentioned? The tug he still felt after having seen the commercial three hundred times? A simple statement, "Kodak would like you to take pictures," is obviously not very meaningful to a viewer. He couldn't care less whether Kodak wants him to take pictures or not; he's only interested in what a picture will do for him. There is no research that tells us what motivates people in this respect. In this area we fly mostly by intuition and judgment. We cannot say to our creative people or anyone else, "Conceive a commercial along these lines; these are the things people like."

Sure, we know they like to see babies. They like to see cats and dogs, and warm, human, cuddly things; but that is not much guidance for a commercial. In this area, we probably had less strategy operating, less of a detailed plan than in most areas of product sell, because this was the wide-open area of *human emotion*.

Let's remember the camera was in there. There was a suggestion that you need a camera, if you're going to take a picture. This was a specific hard item people recognize as a means to an end. People have to buy it if they are going to take a picture. We can find out more about why and when they *buy a camera*, and on what occasions — when they have their first baby, when they get married, or whatever — than we can about when they choose to *take that camera off the shelf and make a picture*.

Because they may buy a camera but leave it on the shelf for a great length of time without taking a picture, we must sell them the idea of taking pictures. We were able to give some support to the question of how "Yesterdays" should be set up, since by now we think we know what seems to force people to take the camera off the shelf, purchase a roll of film, and take a picture. Here we fall back on people's feelings, probably the most important ingredient in the success of this commercial. Frankly, it is the most important ingredient for the success of any account person — rather than any system or any procedure — an appreciation of what people feel.

The key to the game is when he knows he has creative people who can take either a general or a specific marketing strategy, or the most limited amount of direction, and perform *on target*. I mean all targets — not just creative effectiveness, which is most important — but the time target and the money target, too. Then he has much less supervising to do. The scarcer he is in some phases of this operation, the better for everyone.

He also has to understand his client personnel. After all, they are going to make the final decisions. The agency *recommends* — "Man proposes, God disposes." He has to understand what they are looking for; what they are expecting; what they can be persuaded to accept — and what they *cannot*. This has to play a part in his judgment all the way along of what product his agency is coming out with.

In the case of "Yesterdays" we fortunately had both areas of personnel operating along lines that produced the best possible commercial. We had creative people able to enjoy the freedom to create. We had client personnel able to understand this creative process and the freedom necessary, without requiring 37 reviews and 47 meetings and 12 sessions where 18 people came along to see whether the cameraman was actually pointing the camera in the right direction.

THE CLIENT

For fifteen years, E. P. "Ted" Genock has been with the Eastman Kodak Company, currently as Director of Broadcast Advertising. Mr. Genock was born in Paris, grew up in London, and has enjoyed a remarkably interesting international business career — which began 40 years ago with British Decca as a recording engineer. He holds an M.A. in Mathematics from Columbia University. From 1936 on, for almost two decades, Mr. Genock was involved with the gathering or producing of news on film for theatre or broadcast use — with the March of Time, Paramount, and TeleNews (forerunner of the U.S. TV networks' major news departments), where he served as editor-in-chief. During World War II, he had a three-year "time-out" as a newspaper correspondent in the Middle and Far East.

In previous chapters, members of the Thompson staff working on the Kodak account have attested to Mr. Genock's fides in the film production field. It is a competence never exercised by telling someone what to do, but by helping him to do it as well as it can possibly be done. Ted Genock's knowledge of his profession is enormous, and so is the range of public service he gives to that profession.

He is, in short, a delightful person to work for, and with:

When you hear talk about "The Client," I always get a funny image, probably because I've read too many novels about advertising, too many magazine articles, too many reports of sessions of Senate Investigation Committees and harsh statements by production people and writers. It is a pretty horrifying sound — "Client"!

Sometimes this is partly due to a problem between agency and advertiser; there *can* be a lack of real contact between the client, and the agency creative group. (I think Wyatte touched upon this when he referred to an area of non-communication.) It is too bad when this happens; a defensive attitude is apt to arise in promoting (and then defending) the creative group concept at Agency presentations. At times, a point is reached where — because of valid product or client reasons — a change is agreed upon. Then the Agency representative must go back to defend the client to the creative group. Bad images can arise through lack of direct contact, explanations and understanding.

I have been very fortunate (possibly because I came out of film production and a news background) that when we started television advertising for Kodak at Thompson, I had closer involvement with the creative and production groups than usual in regular client relationships.

I have worked with Granger Tripp now for almost 15 years. Granger is one of nature's great gentlemen. More than that, he is a great creative man. More than that, he is a great *director* of creative people — and this is important.

I mention this because when we're talking about client/agency relationships, we're *really* talking about philosophy. There is an area in which you have to leave creative people a great freedom and range of thought and expression. You have to nurture that atmosphere.

It's very important to do this; clients generally do not realize the leverage that exists in this phase of their advertising production. You can buy television time. You can get efficient commercial "reach" and "frequency," but you can also forget the Equation of Communication: that in order to get maximum results from your audience you need a capital "*I*" — a certain value of *Impact* built into your commercial. This Impact factor can vary from a low value to an all-time high in various commercials. It has greater influence than any buying for "reach," "frequency" or "cost per minute." *In TV commercials, "the message is the medium!"*

As a client I have an overriding challenge; whenever there is a commitment for television, it must not appear finally as a "*cost*." It is most certainly an "*investment*," and we expect a return on that investment. Quite evidently, it's going to offer a greater return when the creative aspect and impact of the commercial makes for maximum effectiveness. All the more reason, therefore, for the advertiser to be careful to offer the proper atmosphere for creative output. This should be the whole environment, in my view, of the agency/client relationship.

I think it necessary to allow great freedom for individual ideas, range of thoughts, and one more thing — the opportunity to experiment. For quite a few years now, we have put aside money in our budget for what we call experimental TV commercials. Some of our best commercials have come out of trying something you couldn't pin down with a formal script. It would start with a new technique, a *new* concept, or *new* equipment which could be used experimentally. Creative people thrive on the ability to search for the *little* "extra" reach for excellence.

What has this got to do with "Yesterdays"? The success of this commercial is due probably more to the *attitude* of everybody concerned with it, than with any other attribute. Not to downgrade the wonderful basic work of Ken Thoren and Mike Cimino — but if you listened carefully, I think you'll find two things came out of each stage of the discussion.

I don't think those things would make you say, "Eureka — I've got the way to make the perfect television commercial!" But if you think back, you will find two essential but intangible elements present in each person involved. Number one — ENTHUSIASM. Number two — PROFESSIONALISM.

Emerson said, "Nothing great was ever achieved without enthusiasm." True in the past, true now — and it will always be true. You've got to have sincere Enthusiasm.

Secondly, I believe very strongly in what I call Professionalism. This isn't a question of having technical degrees — or ten to fifteen years' experience. I define Professionalism as "meticulous attention to the smallest detail." If you look back, you'll agree Mike Cimino is the acme of Professionalism in these terms. Not a detail was overlooked by him. Think of the work he went to on the snapshots. Each of those old pictures reenacted, yet with the feeling they were made all through the years.

Think of Ken Thoren. The beginning of all of Ken's scripts have a lovely little capsule summary (*see Appendix B*), that gives both psychological background and a little characterization of the people involved. It supplies the motivation, it gives the whole basic idea; a great help in unifying everybody's ideas on what the commercial is intended to do. This was true too, of Jimmy Fagas, figuring how to segué from old-time music to new. A kitten on the keys gave him the clue, but only because he was thinking *all* the time.

Professionalism in this sense yields the final dividends. It is a little final search for excellence by each in his own particular area. It is also a combination of efforts — because production of a television commercial is probably the most complicated, coordinated, cooperative effort — both in Science and Art — that you can find.

I think it can be said that Professionalism is the last-ditch stand of Excellence. There is almost a mathematical axiom here that the "whole is greater than its parts." Take the little extra work each person along the creative production chain performed and put it all together; they do not add *arithmetically* — they *multiply*. It's *geometric*, because each person was so anxious to do his very best in the area for which he was responsible.

"What can a client do?" I think what a client can do is protect his advertising investment by establishing an atmosphere in which creativity can thrive. He should express opinion, but keep an open mind during and after full discussion of any concept. Being a part of the final decision does not mean being obdurate; neither does it mean having no position nor viewpoint. It *does* mean being concerned that all viewpoints and ideas are expressed, to insure everyone the chance to move out as far as they wish into areas that represent an "extra" search for excellence.

About "Yesterdays," I think Wyatte explained this was not a "new" commercial idea. It was a wonderful, fresh, creative approach to an idea that really goes way back. If you ask "Where did the seed come from?", I think you'd have to go back to George Eastman himself — the importance of the mood, of nostalgia; the motivational fact that sentiment and love are expressed in family snapshots; the latent lethargy in most of us about *taking* the pictures. These are the basic ingredients. If you want to come closer to the era of television, we would have to give credit to Eastman Kodak's former Director of Advertising, Peter Potter. Many years ago he felt something highly motivational could be made in this way. Over the years, he collected pictures of his daughter, and of Jim McGhee's — our Marketing Director's — family, for this purpose.

The TV commercial really started when Granger Tripp heard a Belafonte song, "Turn Around." Almost coincidentally, he received a series of pictures from a Dr. Ellis in Beverly Hills of his daughter Judy, taken from childhood to motherhood. We had the elements we were looking for, we agreed to go ahead — and the classic commercial "Turn Around" was born.

That commercial was the first of a series: "Turn Around"; then "The Way You Look Tonight"; then "Sunrise-Sunset"; and now "Yesterdays." Each covered in a similar way the whole area of motivation for picture-taking — and each has a happy, *optimistic* climax. It's one thing to say "save your pictures" because time passes speedily, but care has to be taken how you express this thought. In a sense you are saying — "You're born — you grow up — you marry." But the next thought is "you die" — not a happy thought for motivational action! So each of these "memories" has a rejuvenation — a return to joy. The payoff in "Turn Around" was, "Turn around, and you're a mother with a babe of your own." The climax of "The Way You Look Tonight" was the Senior Prom — the retrospective snapshot memories were worked into a theme with further expectations. In the case of "Sunrise-Sunset," it was the wedding — a high point and moment of further promise. In the motivation of memories, there is a very narrow road to travel. We call an overly-rapid memory-track the "tombstone approach!" Go *too* far and *too* fast — and the basic motivational appeal of picture-taking can be lost. The total theme must represent the triumph of optimism over pessimism.

Matt Harlib mentioned the fact that the agency producer was a "contractor" to the "architect." Another analogy allows the client to be involved; the agency producer is the *conductor of a symphony*. He is watching and organizing everything to get the finest performance and results from everybody concerned. The client plays the role of a music reviewer; a critic looking at the total picture and its potential — appreciating, lauding and always urging that "search for excellence," that little extra effort. And that effort is usually forthcoming when everyone feels his talent is appreciated and his potential highly regarded.

NOTE: The questions and discussion that followed this presentation appear on p. 151 ff.

Appendix A

Discussion

The I.R.T.S. TV Commercial Production Workshop that yielded the material gathered in this volume took place at Radio City's Johnny Victor Theater in New York City, from January 21st to March 11th, 1969.

Following each panel discussion, a question period offered Workshop participants an opportunity to explore the comments of the panelists in greater detail. Their questions and the replies are transcribed below:

PRINTING & DISTRIBUTION

Q. *In controlling color, what about engineers at the various stations? Do* THEY *correct color of a print? Can they do that?*

MR. LEIGHTON: Well, they can affect it. But normally, with a one-minute commercial — in this case two minutes — coming in off a show, they don't have too much time. So they will normally not correct a commercial; or if they are shading a commercial (they call it "pedestal" control), they will do it over a gradual period, so they would hope you wouldn't see them making the change. But we put the commercial on correctly, and we more or less demand that they project it the way we want them to.

MR. AHTO: The color corrections made in film are made between cuts or between scenes. This is the way the equipment is designed. If you are watching color film on television and you see a sweeping color change that seems to slowly creep up on you between two or three scenes, yes, someone's turning the dial. This is the way you'll recognize the difference.

MR. ANDERSON: There's a difference very often between the color standard that's used for the commercial, and the color standard used for the program material. So you will find engineers "searching" for an answer very often when a commercial comes up.

MR. DIAMANT: It seems fair to say that the whole point of the operation you've discussed, on this particular account, is to try to make it unnecessary for a TV station engineer to ever have to use any subjective judgment whatsoever — or to "outthink" the client, as it were.

Q. *There was discussion about having the projection facilities at the Agency match the projection facilities at the film laboratory. There seems to be a third set of facilities equally important — that of the network. When the commercial is aired, isn't it important to have the same kind of projection there that you've approved?*

MR. LEIGHTON: Well, they project into a tube, and send it out on the air. They are not projecting onto a reflective screen as we have been doing in this theatre. They have matched their facilities to actually throw back what we see on the film. What happens from there on in, when it gets out on the air and into the home receiver, is another matter.

Q. *Once the release prints are made, do you make a periodic check every twenty prints or so, after the release print order is given? And do you check any of the prints "on air"?*

MR. LEIGHTON: We don't check them on air. I do monitor the print orders, and if it's a large print order — if we're printing in the hundreds — I will have them send over every twenty-fifth print or so. As to what would stop them from just pulling off the first five prints and showing them to me — a negative picks up wear while it is being printed, and I've looked at enough prints to evaluate the wear in the first five prints as against the last five.

MISS SOMERS: Also, you usually have to supply a new set of prints for just about every airing, when you get to the network level. There are some shows — like news shows — that don't require this, but if you are on any kind of a film program, you have to supply new material for each airing. There are times when you can re-use prints, but on the Kodak account particularly, we prefer to supply new material as much as possible.

Q. *Do you view these "on system"? That is, not necessarily on the air dates, but do you see these on a television monitor before they are actually put on the network?*

MR. DIAMANT: Closed circuit?

MISS SOMERS: In some cases, but not generally, I would say. We have a department to make sure the correct commercial is on, particularly for a live show like the "Tonight" or "Today" shows. There is someone from the Agency there, and if they see either the wrong commercial, or a very bad quality commercial being run on the monitor, they will of course make sure that new prints are supplied.

MR. DIAMANT: The whole purpose of the "China Girl" lab standard we discussed earlier is to take into account what you ask, and to set up the print, not for reflective theater projection density, but for the best kind of projection you can get on the television tube; and to try to stick to those standards.

MR. ANDERSON: We don't actually screen every commercial on system before we run it. Many we do, but it's not a standard part of our procedure to screen it on system, in answer to your question. I think some of us would prefer in the future to do that. It's expensive. It's time-consuming, and you have to have a lot of equipment available in order to screen every account's material on system all the time.

MR. DIAMANT: At the end of these sessions, instead of seeing "Yesterdays" on direct projection as you have, we'll ask NBC to feed it through a color monitor, so you'll be able to verify that the colors you're seeing on the screen *are* the ones that are coming through a correctly balanced monitor . . . which is a completely different nest of snakes.

Q. *"Wonderful World of Color" is produced on film and "Yesterdays," I guess, was cut right into the show before it went on? With "The Academy Awards," a live show, Kodak commercials come up at certain points. A third situation would be film commercial insertion into a show shot on video tape. What provisions do you make and what differences are there in what you do, to suit your commercials to those three (and maybe more) contingencies?*

MISS SOMERS: Well, if you're talking about quality, we go by our general quality level. We supply prints in what we consider to be superb quality, which should come over well on any system that the network happens to have set up for a particular program. We have to determine in advance, of course, what material they need, and as you pointed out, there are many different kinds of programs. This can get enormously complicated when you're going into one of these "scatter" plan type of buys, where you're on twenty-five or thirty different programs, all with different deadlines, different fines, different quantity requirements — everything is different. You find out from the network well in advance what type of show you're going into, and exactly what their requirements are. They may sometimes require just two "35's." We supply standard color 35's, assuming that their projection will carry through the quality directly. Going into a show like "Wonderful World of Color," we inserted the commercials in positive form — they were cut into positive prints of the program. You could also go into a program at an earlier stage, going into the negative, which is more costly and much more time-consuming. You have to have your prints there as much as a month, or at least three weeks, ahead of the air date.

Q. *What did you do with "Wonderful World of Color"?*

Mr. DIAMANT: Was that positive integration?

Miss SOMERS: That was positive, yes. I think NBC, generally speaking, does all positive insertions.

Q. *It's your show, though. You were in on it right from the beginning. But you didn't cut in negative? You still stayed with positive integration?*

Miss SOMERS: Yes. We didn't touch the show negative on that show at all. NBC just doesn't operate most of their programs that way. ABC does.

Mr. DIAMANT: Isn't the reason for that that a lot of ABC shows are "DB's"; if you can put the commercial negative into the negative of the show, you can strike sixty DB's in one run, and you're done? But NBC doesn't have quite that same programming and affiliate set-up.

Miss SOMERS: Yes. We're on an ABC show now that has a much larger requirement for prints, and we decided in this case, because of the cost of supplying prints just for this one show, it would be much better if we supplied them with a track, an interpositive and a sample print. They have what they call a "negative insert roll"; they strike on a single roll all the prints they require, and they edit that into prints of the show. For quality purposes, we give them an additional set of prints for their network origination, so that we're as sure as we can be that the quality is still going to be excellent. Because on the program prints that will be supplied from the negative insert roll, we'll be another generation away from our original quality. So we make sure that the network gets first generation prints.

Mr. ANDERSON: A further answer to that: I think we, with Kodak's agreement, don't try to make any special prints for a tape show. We set up our standard and supply the same run of prints to all types of shows, including tape and live.

Q. *Film prints are not transferred to tape, as part of a tape special?*

Mr. ANDERSON: Oh, yes. The network itself does that. In fact, they do it a great deal of the time.

Mr. DIAMANT: There's no question that most of the network shows are now on computerized tape. This is to avoid any hangups in transmission and have everything in the right place.

MR. AHTO: What I think you are looking for is the experience I have had. That in many instances, the network will take film commercials furnished by us into a "makeup room," and put together all the film commercials for a given day's shows, and then transfer this to tape. Then the tape is triggered by a computer to come in at a certain time of day.

Q. *In terms of color correction, I assume you refer to correcting "answer prints." Hopefully many of the scenes will be satisfactory; only a few will need to be improved. For instance in "Yesterdays," there are forty-two scenes. Presumably only a few had to be corrected. Now, would you correct from a negative?*

MR. LEIGHTON: All corrections are made with the negative, but you use the last print "off" as your guide for the corrections.

Q. *You said it took about fifteen months to make this commercial. Can you break that down?*

MR. DIAMANT: Come to six more sessions. (Laughter)

MR. ANDERSON: The "fifteen months" was from the time "Yesterdays" was written to the time it went on the air. But there are a lot of stages in there where you're not necessarily doing anything. Maybe the script is sitting up at Kodak, being approved, for instance.

Q. *You also mentioned that "Yesterdays" had been aired only three or four times. Is that all?*

MR. ANDERSON: It was shown twice in '67; twice in '68. It will be shown a number of times in '69.

MR. DIAMANT: I would guess, though, it's been seen hundreds of times around the world in TV festivals . . .

MR. ANDERSON: Yes, it's been shown more in festivals than anywhere else, and we have a room — I'm being facetious — full of statues for "Yesterdays."*

scene 39

scene 42A

Q. *You mentioned that you stay with commercials from the time they're written 'till the time they're finished forever because the product goes out of existence. You say you're going to schedule "Yesterdays" a couple of times this year. Isn't the "Instamatic 104" no longer an item Kodak is making?*

MR. ANDERSON: Very perceptive! (Laughter) I was examining "Yesterdays" today myself with some interest, to see how we could replace that one scene (*scene 39*) in close-up.

MR. DIAMANT: That will require re-shooting?

MR. ANDERSON: Yes. And the final product scene will have to be replaced, too. (*scene 42A*)

*Not too facetious. See Frontispiece. — *Ed.*

MR. TENNYSON: May I make one point? When we discuss the long history of the commercial, the "fifteen months" — needless to say, it isn't that we were continually working on it or trying to get the thing done. There were many decisions to make. *Two-minute* commercials, perhaps, were phasing out, as we thought of other kinds of Kodak programming where *minutes* would be involved. So there were considerations on whether it would be economically feasible to make a *two-minute* with a very limited life, as opposed to other story lines that would work in minutes. The "fifteen months" were the result of many, many decision changes, and by the time we went into a studio and started to actually produce "Yesterdays," the process was cut down to a much more normal length of time.

SOUNDTRACK COMPLETION

MR. DIAMANT: Sol almost called the mixing engineer — and I think it would be true to call him that — a psychiatrist. That's one of his functions. He's got a number of very excitable, involved people sitting there. I was speculating as Sol spoke, on the reason for all that tension; a mixing studio can, at times, be an extremely tense place. I think one of the reasons may be that this is really the last time anyone has a chance to "fool around." At that point you're launching the ship; it's the last whack of the champagne bottle over the bow. After that, you're out on the water, on film, and people have to like it or not like it. But at that point, it's the last moment at which you can still make some kind of correction.

MR. HARLIB: It's also the last major expense in the production of a film commercial. If you're wrong and you have to go back, someone's going to have to eat a lot of money.

Q. *What do you mean by lyric parody?*

MISS PRESTON: If you change the copyright lyrics of a composition — if, for example, instead of using the word "Yesterday," we submitted the word "tomorrow, and tomorrow, and tomorrow" — that would be a parody lyric. Parody lyrics can either mention the client's product, the client, or be a non-advertising type change. If you change the lyric writer's lyrics, then you always have to get approval from the publisher, at least, and sometimes from the composer. You have no right to change the lyrics of a composition without approval. If you use parody lyrics, and if they are advertising lyrics — for example, if Kodak or Instamatic Cameras, whatever, had been mentioned in the song — then the ASCAP performance credits would be very, very much less. This is a consideration when a publisher negotiates a license fee, because part of the value he is getting is his ASCAP credits. We're paying a per-use rate for "Yesterdays," but in addition, every network use of this commercial gives the publisher and the estate of each of its two composers ASCAP credits.

MR. DIAMANT: Does everybody here know what ASCAP credits are?

MISS PRESTON: Let me explain. Briefly, ASCAP is the American Society of Composers, Authors and Publishers, and it is a performing rights society. BMI — Broadcast Music, Inc. — is another performing rights society. SESAC is another, But the two primary ones in the U. S. are ASCAP and BMI. Composers are members of one or the other, not members of both. Publishers are members of one or the other . . . again, not both. Now you may have a composer who may be an ASCAP publisher, and his wife a BMI writer, and this is one way of getting into both houses. Some publishing company groups own both BMI and ASCAP houses, depending upon whom their composers are. Publishers and composers register and sign up with BMI, or with ASCAP, and there's a very complicated formula as to how their *credits* are compiled. An oversimplified explanation is, it depends upon the kind of use. For network usage, every single musical composition, whether in a program or in a commercial, is logged by the network and an accounting is sent regularly to BMI or ASCAP. (I don't know whether it's monthly or quarterly.) As for local stations, ASCAP has a random sampling system. They take, at random, "X" number of stations for radio and "Y" number of stations for television, and they actually record the compositions used within a given period of time. It goes through a complicated process in which uses are projected. If you have had "N uses" in a market within a certain period of time, mathematically that's projected so that nationwide, you end up with "M uses." And those uses are translated into dollars, and composers and publishers receive dollars from ASCAP and BMI, based upon the performance of their compositions. And for major writers — your Jerome Kerns, your Irving Berlins, your Richard Rodgers' — these credits run into very sizable amounts of money. So that composers are very often willing to make a sacrifice on the initial license fee, in exchange for the network credits that they will be getting.

MR. DIAMANT: "Yesterdays" has been used exclusively on network. Was any sacrifice made in this case?

MISS PRESTON: No. The copyrighted lyrics were so much a part of the creative idea that the publisher — Stan Stanley, representing T. B. Harms — would not agree to any kind of a reduced payment. We're paying for the lyrics as an extremely important part of this commercial. In another case, where we might be buying just background music, and you could use any composition, with no tie-in with the words as in this case — "Yesterdays" representing a complete tie-in with the whole concept — then we probably could have arranged a lower payment.

Q. *A question about sequence: Sol said everything as far as mixing is concerned is done by footage, rather than by clock time. Some place along the line somebody had to determine the length of time, or the amount of footage, that — for instance — the announcer's copy would take. This has to coincide with the visual things taking place. What do you do first?*

MR. HARLIB: You get a script first. The script pretty much lays out what's going to happen and when. Those are your plans, your architectural drawings. Then everything else from there on is compromise and fight, to solve all of the problems posed by the architectural drawings. For example, we know that in this particular case — it was easy — the song used up so much time, at such and such a tempo. So we had a minute and some-odd seconds to tell a certain part of the story. Then we had another period of time, determined by what was left from the two-minute length, to tell another part of the story — and another segment of time to squeeze in the announcer's part, which, fortunately, was only twenty-two words long. The rest of it is a combination of balance, judgment, intuition, feel, and fight with other people who want more time in one place than another. For instance, the director shot an opening scene that doesn't even exist in the final film. It's on the cutting-room floor. He shot a complete entrance to the attic that involved a lot of dialogue, that ran for about 30 seconds before the music started, and he felt that "Yesterdays" should open that way, and that things at the other end should have been sacrificed, rather than the way it finally wound up. Very early in the game, that was compromised.

It was decided at a production meeting to let him shoot it that way, and we would take a look at it on the Moviola, and let him make a "cut" and see it his way, and then make changes from that . . . which is what was done.

MR. DIAMANT: But it's not the sound mixer's decision, at his console, to make anything more than the most minute readjustments. The basic determination of what falls where is made before the mix materials come to Sol.

MR. HARLIB: Well, are you referring only to the music, or to the entire structure of the sound?

Q. *I'm referring to all of the elements that go into the film. For instance, you say you know how long the music takes. It would seem to me that that would be quite a flexible thing. Surely Jimmy could play a portion of the music in 18 seconds; or could he play it in 21 seconds?*

MR. HARLIB: One of the first steps when the script was written was to get a recording of "Yesterdays," and time it. There were so many bars, and so many notes.

Q. *So in this case you started with an arbitrary recording that you wanted to use?*

MR. HARLIB: We got a recording *circa* 1935, and listened to it, and said "This is the tone," the tempo of the time. You see, everything in "Yesterdays" is faithful to the basic idea of an old recording and photographs that brought memories to the fore. To start, we got an actual record, and asked Jimmy to duplicate its musical sound. So that determined the length.

MR. TABACHNICK: This commercial was a pre-score, am I right? It was "shot" audio-wise — before it was laid together?

MR. FAGAS: There was a "scratch track" made.

MR. TABACHNICK: That's what I mean. In other words, you planned the commercial around a scratch track. It wasn't shot, and then you laid the track against the picture.

MR. HARLIB: A scratch track could be a piano track. It could be somebody humming.

MR. DIAMANT: It's correct to *time*, but to nothing else. It's a guide to filming.

MR. HARLIB: Actually, the final sequence of pictures used against the lyric was not determined until people began looking at it on the Moviola. A lot of material was available to be shaped and sculpted, but was never used in the film at all. The final cut took months and months, with many, many revisions.

MR. DIAMANT: We're working our way backwards — up the river, so to speak — and soon we'll be at the Moviola stage of "Yesterdays," where you do things that seem logical, discover fortuitous combinations that just happen to be right, and you grab them. Other things seem terribly wrong, and you go home at night wondering how you're going to straighten it out the next day. But that's long before it gets into Sol's hands, and gets racked up on his dubbers.

MR. HARLIB: Sol didn't give himself enough credit; he was being too modest. It's not just a question of "footage," because if you're dealing with a cue sheet with eight tracks, reading them in sixty seconds, and some of them coming in and out every second, or every two seconds, and you're riding levels on all those channels so that the ultimate blend does not jar you, but rather happens smoothly and seems not to have been thought about at all — then you're a pretty busy guy, because not only are you reading the footage marks on the cue sheet, but you're reading the footage counter directly under the screen, and you're looking at the picture, and you're listening to the words and trying to see and do everything at the same time . . . you sometimes wish you were an octopus. It's not just mechanical skill.

MR. TABACHNICK: There is one thing I did leave out, and Matt just brought it up. There are many times when you get into such a bind that you do a "pre-mix." If the track becomes so complicated, you'll take one element, like four different music tracks that have to be segued — and during those segués you have other complicated moves going on — then you'll pre-mix those elements into a single track, and this will give you more freedom and latitude later on. In "Yesterdays," it wasn't necessary, because most of the movements that were required were not combined. You had a few half-seconds here and there to move your hands and your eyes around. But a lot of times, there are commercials where you have to pre-mix three-quarters of the commercial in order to get the control you need.

MR. HARLIB: Then there are other factors that go into a music mix, such as: shall you leave more "top" on the music — more "highs" — or shall you put more bottom into it — more "lows"? Make it sound a little heavier, rather than lighter? Are trumpets blasting into the voice, when you want them kept *under* the voice? How much do you want the voice and music coming together, or separated? These are all decisions that mixers make most of the time without even bothering the agency people or anybody, because it only raises more questions than they care to see raised, often with the client present. If the question comes up, of course, they'll get into it.

MR. DIAMANT: Jimmy, did you give Thompson a completely mixed track, or separate music tracks?

MR. FAGAS: A mixed track.

MR. DIAMANT: You may sometimes — once all the other elements are heard against the music — want to re-balance the music mix. Incidentally, the latest RCA Records mixing console for music recording has 28 channels, manned by three engineers at once. That's the way an orchestral mixing session can use up equipment and human ability. Very few commercials reach that level, but if they do, the mixing studio has to be equipped to handle them. That's the purpose of the pre-mix, because then an individual engineer can break down sections of the mix by himself.

MR. TABACHNICK: Most of the things we have mentioned apply to New York. In most studios here, one man will handle up to ten tracks. If you go out to Hollywood, because of certain union regulations, one man will not be allowed to handle more than three tracks. So if you have a complicated commercial, you're now raising the mixing cost on the Coast. We have done a few commercials where we have had two men on the mix; would you believe a one-minute commercial with 22 tracks! And they wouldn't premix; they wanted to do it live! So naturally, if they were willing to absorb the cost, we were happy to supply the manpower and equipment. But basically in New York, most of your commercial work is done by one man. He will mix all the tracks. And of course your projectionist and dubber is still required. Again, with 22 tracks and two mixers, your dubber room requires two men, and you're adding to your costs.

Miss Preston: It occurs to me that I didn't mention where ASCAP and BMI get their money to pay publisher and composer members. ASCAP negotiates licenses with radio stations, television stations, and the radio and television networks. Obviously, all the networks have licenses with ASCAP, and they pay a certain dollar amount based on — I'm not sure whether it's gross income, or time sales. But there is a formula for determining what the license fee is. ASCAP and BMI have performing rights contracts with most radio and television stations throughout the United States. However, not 100%; there are some stations which will *not* enter into a licensing agreement with ASCAP. The problem with those stations is that if you have ASCAP music in your commercials, they cannot play those commercials, or else they run the risk of being sued.

Q. *I work in station promotion, and our station, of course, has a license for both ASCAP and BMI. Can I then use any of their records in promotion work, without further payment?*

Miss Preston: If you have an ASCAP license, then I really think you ought to talk to the people who handle that area.

Q. *But I've been doing what I said. Nobody even complained.* (Laughter)

Mr. Diamant: *Careful! We're on tape!* (Laughter)

Miss Preston: I don't want to give you a legal interpretation of your contract, but I would be very surprised if it indicates certain kinds of ways you can use ASCAP music and precludes other kinds. But you really should check with the person who negotiated your contract.

THE EDITING PROCESS

Q. *The edited workprint that you get; is that all on one reel? If so, what, what is all this "A" and "B" nonsense my editors keep giving me, every time I want to get a dissolve, or something like that?*

Mr. Fineman: Assume you want a scene that's going to require double exposure. There are different ways of handling this. Often we try to overlay the prints — one image right on top of the other — running that double thickness through the Moviola, so we can visualize the effect. In laying out the optical work, we set up the scenes on an "A" and a "B" roll, and the optical bench man uses edge numbers to know where each scene takes place: knowing at what point to fade up, at what point to drop exposure, at what point to come back to normal exposure — and still maintaining the correct running footage in sequence.

High-contrast title   and mate

Q. *"A" and "B" rolls would not be part of the workprint?*

Mr. Fineman: Running that particular effect in the early stages, as we're trying to visualize it for the producer or the agency people or the client or whoever wants to see it, it's much easier, as I said, to run it through the Moviola in a double thickness. But laying out the job for the optical house, we give that workprint to him as "A" and "B" rolls.

Q. *Is there any difference in the subject matter on those "A" and "B" rolls?*

Mr. Fineman: Of course. Assuming a double exposure, the master scene would be running on the "A" roll, with the scene that double-exposed over it, on the "B" roll.

Mr. Diamant: Are *two* rolls to be sure that — in the case of a two-minute spot — you start your optical frame count at "0" on each roll, and end at 2,880 on each roll, with everything in proper position?

Mr. Pittluck: Right. The layout man runs through the "A" and "B" roll workprints against his interpositives, identifying them and marking his scene "start" and "end" points.

Q. *Sometimes I've had numbers on a "A" roll and picture material on a "B" roll, and the numbers were fuzzy, and they said, "They must have printed those from the 'B' roll instead of the 'A' roll . . ."*

Mr. Fineman: Do you mean *edge* numbers?

Q. *No. Visual numbers.*

Mr. Diamant: I think you're talking about "A-wind" and "B-wind."

Mr. Fineman: Yes, that's a different story. That relates to final printing; in 16mm, more than in 35mm.

Mr. Pittluck: We're confusing something here. In the case of this commercial, no printing was done from *original* material, once we get beyond the dailies and interpositives. In 16mm work, very often where the effects are very simple, "A" and "B" rolls are set up as alternate scenes, and running it through the printing machine one pass is printed from the "A", the film is rewound, and the second pass is printed from the "B", making dissolves from one to the other as you go through. This technique is used occasionally in 35mm for straight work, but it wasn't involved in this spot. As for "A-wind" and "B-wind", that refers to which way original film material "reads" — whether it is projected with the emulsion or the base towards the lens.

Mr. Fineman: "Yesterdays" could have been cut as an "A" and "B" roll negative — if you don't count the superimposed titles — since there were no dissolves. But this would have meant taking the original camera negative and actually chopping it into little pieces to match the workprint, and this would have made those scenes unusable in the future for anything else. So while a simple spot does permit doing this, it spoils the negative for any further uses. Often on Kodak, we want to re-use other parts of scenes we've used a year or so ago. If we had cut those scenes up — which would save a generation, incidentally, on the final print — we would have wasted thousands of dollars (and time) invested in original camera work to make it available for just one commercial.

Q. *How did you lay that "Kodak" logo into the final film? (scene 1)*

MR. PITTLUCK: It takes several pieces of film. One is the interpositive of the background scene. Another is a black high-contrast "Kodak" outline that holds back that area . . .

MR. DIAMANT: May I interrupt a moment? We start, am I right, with a piece of type? We set the work "Kodak" in type (or take the artwork of the logo), and then we photograph that in the exact size and position that we want it in the final frame?

MR. PITTLUCK: Those are the first steps. Now we have the interpositive without the "Kodak," and a high contrast piece of film with nothing but the black letters "Kodak" on it, and we have a mate to that, which has the white title "Kodak" on it.

MR. FINEMAN: And when this "Kodak" is filmed, it is placed before the camera and photographed in the correct position it will occupy in the film. We decide in advance where we want to put it — usually in a position where it doesn't bother any action of the scene, because it's just there for identification. So when they re-photograph the interpositive onto a piece of dupe negative, they do it with the black "core" which (as Bob explained) is going to hold back the section of the scene where the white title is going to appear, and than wind back, and photograph the white title, offsetting it slightly to get a "drop-shadow" effect.

MR. PITTLUCK: And if the title was in color, we would use a filter to put in the color.

Q. *What is the meaning of "interpositive," "positive," "internegative," "negative"?*

MR. FINEMAN: "Positive" is a direct print off the original negative. "Interpositive" is a special fine-grain base stock that will retain all the lighting characteristics, color values and densities in the original negative (ordinary positive daily stock will not hold these). This stock is used to make the optical negative. It is more expensive than daily stock.

MR. PITTLUCK: The "inter" stands for "intermediate" — the stock is designed as an intermediary step between the original negative and the final negative. Again, an "internegative" is an intermediate negative. It so hap-

scene 1

pens that the intermediate positive stock and the intermediate negative stock are the same stock.

MR. DIAMANT: I would guess that the formulation of the emulsion is different from daily print stock, to take more wear?

MR. PITTLUCK: Yes. The intermediate stock is essentially processed the same as the original camera stock, whereas the print stock is processed entirely differently.

Q. *I gather the original camera negative is different stock than what a TV newsman shoots, processes, and puts on the air the same night?*

MR. DIAMANT: Yes. He's shooting "reversal" film.

MR. PITTLUCK: They are currently using Ektachrome Reversal for a lot of news.

MR. DIAMANT: With reversal, what eventually gets projected is the same piece of film that originally went through the camera. The color values are reversed. Whereas with "Yesterdays," we had several pieces of film, all of them doing one basic thing — protecting the investment in the original camera negative material, so it could be used over and over again in whatever ways become necessary.

Q. *Why did you finally go to the attic? Was it to get the shot of Grandpa throwing the football, or was it for a more "sympatico" scene. We've heard about this controversy a couple of times.*

MR. ALDORETTA: That was a purely personal thing. I can give you a lot of reasons, but they would all be personal. Mike Cimino and I both felt very strongly for the attic and against the basement. One reason was that the basement would not have given us much of an overhead to work with. We would have had a very low area, and the heat on the set would have built up enormously. Another thing was we felt we could get a great deal more charm out of the architecture. The wood could open us up into all sorts of different designs, with windows. There was more room for props; we could put skis up on top of the ceiling, and do all sorts of things with hanging lamps, antique lamps. . . .

Q. *I couldn't agree with you more. Why was the writer fighting for the basement? There's no charm to a basement.* (Laughter)

MR. DIAMANT: I'm going to foreclose that question until we get into the CREATIVE area — where the writer will have a chance to defend himself!

MR. ALDORETTA: When he's here, he may fight harder for the basement!

MR. DIAMANT: You can see that beside the purely mechanical aspects of an editor's job, his *taste* — when he makes his moves, *when* he makes his cuts, what he's looking for, what little nuance he's trying to develop — is terribly important. I was curiously surprised to hear the iced tea story. I've looked at "Yesterdays" many times; I always thought Grandpa was carrying a can of beer. Now I discover it's a glass of iced tea.

MR. FINEMAN: No, he is carrying a can . . . of soda, which is in a later point in the spot. The iced tea sequence had a little dialogue along with it, when she first came up the steps.

Q. *Were you planning to use that dialogue as opening conversation?*

MR. FINEMAN: Originally, yes. There was a little bit of Grandma's dialogue that would have come in — he was all irate about having dropped the trunk — such as "Have a little drink to cool you off," but there was no room, so we had to cut around it. So when she has come up the steps we keep away from the iced tea and the pitcher as much as possible in the editing, so it loses itself completely.

MR. ALDORETTA: The way Mike Cimino works, he takes acting very seriously; he's been taking acting courses for quite a while. What he does when he works with actors and actresses is to give them improvised little scenes to work out. It relaxes them and puts them into a role they can really lose themselves in, where they become free of inhibition and self-consciousness. I think it does a fantastic job.

Q. *One of the most interesting things I think an editor can do is to play tricks with time. We had the feeling we were in the attic a full hour, even though the film was very brief (and of course the actors were there all day long). But by judiciously cutting away and back, the editing gives the feeling we've been there all the time. Doesn't it take a good deal of skill to do that and avoid "jump cuts," that look like mistakes?*

MR. FINEMAN: Tightening this up, you have to make every cut that wasn't planned in the camera *work*. This becomes quite a job, at times. You've seen some commercials where editors are so stymied by a cut that won't "cut," so they resort to the good old-fashioned *dissolve,* to bridge a bad action. The trick, if the footage is there, is always to try to make the cut without having to use an optical gimmick.

MR. ALDORETTA: Another thing George added to the entire concept: Our mood was beginning to get so intense with the fact that these people were looking back into their past life, unable to recapture youth — that we were beginning to get a little bit morbid. What George did at that point was to inject an edited smile. You'll notice there's a place there where Grandma laughs very brightly; it just breaks up that whole grim mood and keeps things positive. (*scene 26*)

scene 26

FILMING THE COMMERCIAL

Q. *Aside from shooting the stills, how many shooting days were required to film the interiors and the exteriors?*

MR. CIMINO: The interior set — the attic set — took two days, with six hours overtime. We used three-quarters of a day doing the live house exterior — an afternoon's shooting. The still work took three or four days of shooting.

Q. *The exterior shots were all shot in the same day?*

MR. CIMINO: The live shots?

Q. *Yes.*

MR. CIMINO: One afternoon. We stopped when the light went. You can already see the light getting a little yellow — a little orange — at the end of the day. It was autumn, so we were working with a shorter day, anyway.

Q. *Is it appropriate to ask about the process of selecting the voice-over announcer?*

MR. ALDORETTA: Anything specific? What went into our final decision on using a particular announcer?

Q. *Yes. Is he an announcer under contract to Kodak, or was there a process of auditioning, or what was the procedure?*

MR. ALDORETTA: We have had a great deal of success with Bob Landers, who was involved here. We have found a great deal of talent around, but when it comes to subtle inflections — little tiny nuances — there aren't really that many people who can bring that sensitivity to a reading. We are continually looking for new talent. Two weeks ago, I must have spent almost three days doing nothing but listening to voices, both men and women —giving them a piece of poetry, as a matter of fact. We were looking for that sensitivity and one of the things we have found is that a man, confronted with expressing emotions and feelings, often feels quite self-conscious and a little embarrassed, and really does not project the warmth and emotion we're looking for. Now this is, of course, a personal thing I have experienced, but we have found that Bob Landers — who is under no special contract with us whatsoever — has brought a great deal of sensitivity to the Kodak tracks.

MR. DIAMANT: That kind of announcer auditioning goes on all the time. Mike shot some Revlon spots for me a year or so ago, and before we got an announcer track on them to satisfy all the cosmetic brass who had to be satisfied, I auditioned 140 announcers, all across the country. The person you end up with can be a surprise. Revlon's was one of the poker players in "The Odd Couple." That's why I like blind auditions — everyone anonymous and reading the same copy; *only* the producer knows who's who when it's played back.

Q. *Why did you use a male announcer, not a female announcer?*

Mr. Aldoretta: A good question. Another good question might be, why did we use a female singer, rather than a man? These things get very involved and very personal. I think the male announcer was more or less counterpoint. Mike mentioned he thought the music was too sweet. I think that with the sensitivity and delicacy of the spot itself and the type of emotion we were creating here, to go along with another woman in the voice-over would have been just too much. If we had used a man — and I'll be honest with you, looking back now I feel that perhaps a male singer would have worked better (that's Monday morning quarterbacking) — then perhaps I would have reversed the situation, and gone the other way.

Mr. Cimino: The problem with doing Kodak commercials is that you're always on the edge of something maudlin. It's very hard to stay on the right side, because you go just a smidgin too far, and it's a mass of corn. It's difficult on Kodak — because of the situation they're dealing with — to give it some edge, some little bit of reality.

Mr. Diamant: I've had the feeling about "Yesterdays" that if there was one false note along the way that obviously looked contrived or phony, the whole idea would have crumbled slightly. That's why all the detail seems so important, even though, as Mike says, much of it never showed up on the tube. But the *feeling* was right, all along.

Q. *Who was responsible for the final scene Mike protested about? Was it a client add-on, or your add-on?*

Mr. Aldoretta: These decisions are never simple. I had my own thoughts on how to end the spot. I usually try to steer clear, as much as I can, from using snapshots at the end of a Kodak commercial. We're coming up with a new approach to this now; we show a man or a woman holding a camera. Then we cut to the action, and we hear the click of the camera, and the action freezes. From there on, if we want to show snapshots — or create the feeling of snapshots being taken — we just show a series of freezes and then even eliminate the click, too, so we have no white borders to deal with, and no click of the camera, but we're saying, "Snapshots are being taken." Today if we had shot this, the ending would have been different. But this was two years ago and these things evolve slowly. But Mike's criticism of the last scene is well taken.

Q. *Did your shooting schedule follow pretty much the sequence of scenes in the completed film?*

Mr. Cimino: Generally, I try for that. Every director likes to shoot in continuity, if it's possible. It's better for the actors, it's better for you, it's better for everyone. You have a greater sense of the progression of what's going on. "Yesterdays" was done, basically, in continuity. Sometimes you can't. Usually, in features or commercials, it can't be done for purely economic reasons — a set has to come down, or somebody's available only on a particular day. But this was done pretty much in continuity.

Q. *If there is ever to be a shorter version of this commercial, whose decision will it be as to what is cut out or altered?*

Mr. Cimino: At this point, it would have nothing to do with me any more. It would probably be up to Thompson's Creative Supervisor on the Kodak account, or to whatever particular producer he assigned to the problem. It might be Warren; it could be somebody else. Usually, what I try to do is to stay with my cutting all the way. I cut with an editor who usually works only with me — Bennet Canarick. I always stay through the cutting and the finishing. I participate in picking the sound effects, the mix — everything. It usually means working around the clock, because you shoot during the day and cut at night. But I think it's essential. *At every step of a film, you're faced with a series of choices, and the minute you leave any choice to somebody else, it reflects not your opinion, it reflects somebody else's, and it subtly changes the film.* It moves it all a half-degree to one side; a number of those changes will move it away from what you want. It happens at every single stage. You look in the camera and you set a certain thing, and somebody nudges the camera — and it changes it. It happens in the editing. If you're interested, you must stay on top of all of those things. In the case of Kodak, I did not participate that much in the editing, because Kodak already has their own editor at MPO — George Fineman — who cuts only Kodak, and is usually up to his neck cutting eight thousand Kodak spots simultaneously. Mainly what I did on "Yesterdays" was to check the first rough-cut George made; I don't normally work that way. Had I cut "Yesterdays," it would probably look quite different. It might not have been as good, but it would have been different.

Q. *How much contact did you have with the client? Or was it mostly with Warren?*

Mr. Cimino: On this particular commercial, it was mostly with Warren. There was an initial meeting with the writer — Ken Thoren — but almost all the contact there on in was with Warren. It was an easy working relationship, a very pleasant one. There are not too many of those, but this one happened that way. Most relationships are battles, right down to the wire.

Q. *Warren, do you often have much contact with the client at shooting sessions?*

MR. ALDORETTA: We really enjoy a unique position in this business, as far as our relationship to our client, Eastman Kodak, goes. We have a very professional group of guys at Thompson who have a beautiful working relationship with the people in Rochester. The man directly responsible there, as far as TV is concerned, is Ted Genock. Ted brings an enormous amount of experience to this area. He could go out and produce one of these commercials any time he wanted to; he is that much of a professional. But he leaves us strictly alone; we have had a fine track record on Kodak, and I think a lot of it is due to the freedom Ted has given us in what we do. We show him a script, we make our recommendations as to whom we feel should produce the spot, and from then on we're strictly on our own. I'm well aware that on many accounts, you have many people — sometimes as many as ten — representing the client at a shooting. But I've been producing on Kodak since the end of 1965, and I have yet to see Ted Genock in a studio or out on location somewhere. It's the same thing with our Thompson people, like Granger Tripp, who is responsible for our contact with Ted. Granger also leaves us strictly alone; it's a beautiful relationship that has worked out well.

MR. CIMINO: It happens that this particular commercial was an unusual working relationship for me, too. Most jobs I've been on have been extraordinary battles, right from the beginning. But this one, for a variety of reasons, went very, very smoothly, and was friendly all the way. I don't know why — it's probably a combination of a lot of factors. This sounds like a lot of sweetness and light, I suppose, all of us praising each other, but it did happen that way. It was really strange; I was surprised it went that smoothly, because as most of you know, it's usually much more of a struggle.

Q. *I wonder if all of you had a lot to do with that? Warren strikes me as a very friendly, rational guy, and there are lots of belligerent people in this business.* (Laughter)

MR. ALDORETTA: Who wants to be rational? (Laughter)

Q. *I mean, in terms of making decisions, and that kind of thing, you can get some guy who says, "Dammit, this is what I want!" Isn't that kind of guy hard to get along with?*

MR. CIMINO: *The single most difficult thing to deal with is a defensive attitude.* When people come on defending something from the beginning, that is probably the single most destructive attitude in any production. When someone feels they have to defend a position or an idea only for the sake of who they are, or to preserve their position — you're dead! On "Yesterdays," the only thing everybody was thinking of was the result. Which is all you should ever think of, but unfortunately, in most cases, it becomes something else. When you have six people defending separate positions; when the account supervisor, the creative director, the producer and the writer all are defending their little avenues of vested interest, it kills you. It kills you. It just clobbers you. It just flattens everything out. But in this case, all we were dealing with was one person — Warren — and he allowed it to "happen." It was no different from a director *allowing* actors within a scene to play it, *allowing* the event to take place. The producer, in a sense, is the director of the larger event that surrounds the smaller event the director is directing. And he has to allow the players within that larger event to somehow play it out. Normally, that does not happen; there's much more interference. And not always for good reasons. Sometimes, for very good reasons, but not always.

MR. ALDORETTA: A case in point is when we were shooting our stills. Mike and I would review contact sheets to see the series of pictures taken the previous day. George Marvin, the Assistant Director, called a lunch break, but Mike and I were so anxious to go over the pictures that we couldn't even think about lunch. So we just sat on the porch up there in Danbury and looked at the whole sheet of pictures, and then Mike said, "That's it," and I said, "That's it," and it was as simple as that. In practically every case we just zeroed right in on the problem together.

MR. CIMINO: We also made Polaroid pictures of all the still set-ups, before we shot them. I think that's an invaluable thing on any production. I use a Polaroid to scout locations, plan my shots, check sets — it's a great way of working. Kubrick uses it extensively on everything he does — checking lighting, checking angles. It's really a great help. From the agency viewpoint, there's always the question, "What's it going to look like? How's it going to look?" which is very often directed to the cameraman or the director by the agency producer or art director. I think it's rather a simple thing to carry a Polaroid around, take your own shots, and see for yourself. Whether it's to check makeup or hair, or see what a set is going to look like from a particular angle, it takes two seconds to snap a Polaroid picture. It's very valuable.

MR. DIAMANT: I don't think Kodak will object to that professional plug for the competition. (Laughter) Particularly since I suspect they're working on an instant-processing camera themselves now. If you do get the feeling that Someone up there was smiling on this entire production, let's ask Mike and Warren to recall an anecdote I overheard when we were sitting around talking and planning these sessions. A bulb exploded over everybody's head during the auditions, and no one was hurt?

MR. CIMINO: We had a long table set up in the studio, covered with the normal pile of composites and "head sheets," and the electricians hung a "cone" directly overhead, hanging straight down — which you're never supposed to do, because that huge bulb can heat up and explode — and no one noticed it. We had everybody dancing around the studio, music playing, and then one actress came in and sat down, and just as she told me her name and handed me her composite, the bulb exploded! There was a shower of flaming glass, flying all over and burning up the composites. People were screaming and running. The studio was in panic. Sixty other actors and actresses who were waiting outside jumped up and ran in. Everyone was dashing around, on fire and what not. My arm was slashed open; I was walking out, bleeding, and in the middle of all of it, this girl was just sitting there saying, "But . . . what about my interview?" (Laughter)

PRE-PRODUCTION & CASTING

Q. *What did you use for dust? Real dust?*

MR. HEUGLIN: No. We used charcoal and fuller's earth, for dark and light dust.*

AGENCY CREATION & PRESENTATION

Q. *How long did it take to do the storyboard? Were there several drafts of it before you reached the final stage?*

MR. TRIPP: Not that I recall. Basically, the way we work is to have the art director rough out — very rough — a series of sketches which are then turned over to a renderer in our art studio. Those original sketches, I am sure, have long since been lost. But Hal first sat down with Ken to rough-out — in art director's shorthand — the basic concept of the storyboard, and then turned it over to our studio within the agency, to complete board; but if you need it tomorrow morning, they'll deliver it tomorrow it. How long did it take? Like many other things in television production, it takes "all the time you've got." They can use a week to make a story-morning, even if they have to work all night. Among many things that make "Yesterdays" an unusual commercial, not only was it part of a continuing creative assignment, but initially we had no firm air date. All we knew was that once we had it in the works, when it was ready we'd put it on the air.

*The length of this Workshop session precluded an extensive question period. — *Ed.*

So we were able to proceed at a rather more leisurely pace than we usually do with most commercials. That's why it took from April 15, 1966 to the initial air date of July 23, 1967 — about a year and a quarter — to get from script to air. That's unusual. It's because we really weren't in any hurry, and certain people were away from time to time, and we just weren't pushing.

Q. *Was the storyboard originally rendered in color?*

Mr. Tripp: Yes. These are photostats. I wish I knew where the originals were; we appear to have lost them. There's really no advantage in doing a storyboard for a color commercial now in anything but color.*

Q. *Ken, I'm just wondering what kind of deadlines you were speaking of when you mentioned you work under deadlines? You mentioned rolling an idea around in your mind for a couple of months before you ever put it down. Is that normal? Are you allowed to take that kind of time to work on an idea?*

Mr. Thoren: Not really, but as Granger pointed out, Kodak has a big "gift push" in the Spring, so we know that so many scripts have to be written and when they have to be shot, to make certain deadlines. And there's a big Christmas push, of course, so that's another big package of plans. Are there any others?

Mr. Tripp: The Academy Awards.

Mr. Thoren: Yes, the Academy Awards. Also, Granger will say, "We need one for the P-14" (that's a still camera). But aside from all those, there are the picture-taking commercials, or as we call them, "motivational" commercials, just to get people thinking about taking pictures of their kids, any day. It's almost a rotating assignment that goes on and on. How many are we doing a year now in this area . . . ? (I'm no longer on the account, so I don't know.)

Mr. Diamant: You got promoted? (Laughter)

Mr. Tripp: About five.

Mr. Thoren: Only five "motivational" commercials a year, so this is why there is this great luxury of mulling over an idea — Granger has a file; he has some good ones in there, yet (Laughter) that have never gone to the client, because it's such a rotating thing. That's why it can take months before a script would even be handed to them. We finished shooting another commercial recently that was written well over a year before, but there was no specific need for it at the time, so it just stayed there, and then finally, when it was needed, it came out of the drawer.

Mr. Tripp: That's unusual, though.

Mr. Thoren: Yes, I guess it is.

*Hal Taylor disagrees. See p. 101. — *Ed.*

Q. *Do you think you could have knocked this out in a couple of weeks if you'd had to?*

MR. THOREN: The idea? That's hard to answer. I'm not sure whether or not it would have been quite the same. The luxury of time wasn't what produced it. Actually, last Fall, Granger came to me and said, "We need a couple of picture-taking commercials for the Academy Awards," and I think we had several good ones within a period of weeks. It's hard to say. If my memory serves, "Sunrise-Sunset" was written under a two-week deadline date. The idea was there, but the shooting was finished and approved in that short time.

Q. *Does Kodak have a "wild spot" schedule on the air?*

MR. TRIPP: Yes.

Q. *Well, when you go to write a Kodak commercial, and you know you need something to put into a big spectacular full-dress program like the "Academy Awards" — do you write a subtly different kind of commercial than if you were writing one for the wild spot schedule?*

MR. THOREN: Yes. A "wild spot" commercial would be a lot more product-oriented — for a specific camera or film — whereas the big "showcase" spots would be written a little softer and more generally, to try to hold as broad an audience as we can.

MR. TRIPP: The length, too, of course, would be different.

Q. *What are the internal mechanics at Thompson for coordinating a Kodak campaign in print and other media with the things that you all are doing in the broadcast media? Is there any kind of effort of that sort?*

MR. TRIPP: It is all coordinated to some extent by virtue of the fact that it is all done within the same group. Some of the creative people work back and forth between print and television, but most of them work primarily in print *or* television. We don't have a strict policing method on coordination; we just try to keep everybody in touch with everybody else. When basic campaigns are requested, they are executed in both media at the same time, and then we try to pull them together. This is another subject, that could take a lot of discussion; I think there are a lot of advantages and disadvantages to a rigid adherence to the same campaign in widely-differing media. It helps to increase impact if you can have a campaign in all media, but the danger in taking a *print* campaign and handing it to a writer, saying, "Here, make a television commercial out of that," is that it just doesn't work. And if it doesn't work, you're better off going separate ways, because the public may not know that it's the same campaign — or care!

Q. *After this commercial was finished, and you went on to other Kodak commercials, did you make any effort to "borrow" any concept from this one that you felt was particularly successful?*

MR. TRIPP: I don't recall any.
MR. THOREN: No.

Q. *Would it make sense to do that sort of thing?*

MR. DIAMANT: Did you see anything specific that you thought might be borrowed?

Q. *Well, the soft sell, and the use of the music, and the appearance of the product only at the very end . . . that sort of thing.*

MR. TRIPP: Oh, yes, in those terms. We have done a great many commercials like that over a period of years — "Yesterdays" was not the first in line — which were frankly designed to evoke emotional response. And when you say that, you're talking about music. So we have done a number of them: "Sunrise-Sunset" was very successful; "The Way You Look Tonight" was very successful. One of the earliest was called "Turn Around." It was actually built from a series of pictures taken by a father of his daughter, over a period of twenty years. That was a real case of taking *actual* pictures and putting them into a commercial. The closing line, "All it takes is a camera, Kodak film and a little thoughtfulness," has been used in a number of commercials, and we continue to use it.

Q. *Was that the first time the line was used — in "Yesterdays"?*

MR. THOREN: No. I guess it was first used in "Turn Around."
MR. TRIPP: You hear many complaints about commercials. These commercials draw a tremendous mail response to Kodak. People write and complain to various government bureaus about comercials. Once Ted Genock asked the FCC, "How many letters do you get in the course of a year, complaining about commercials?" I forget what their number was — it wasn't as many as you think — a few hundred, perhaps. But Ted had received more letters in praise of "Turn Around" during the course of that year than the FCC had received in complaint about all other U. S. commercials combined! *So the idea that the public is ready to rise up in righteous indignation against commercials is exaggerated.*

Q. *Of the 30 frames in the storyboard, only about 4 appear to be devoted to the sequence where Kodak actively sells the product. But when it was translated to the screen, almost a quarter of the commercial was devoted to "picture-taking" sell. Was this originally intended to be a briefer area, or was that just storyboard shorthand?*

scene 34A

scene 37

MR. THOREN: As Granger pointed out, that's one of the faults of a storyboard. When we finally shot "Yesterdays" and got into editing, we found out the "sell" had to run as long as it did, to make sense. That shot of Grandpa upstairs throwing down the football (*scene 34A*) represented days of agony, because the commercial was cut so tight it looked like he threw it and came shooting out the front door the next moment. (*scene 37*) There is a "cutaway" there now, but it still looks as if he had to shinny down a fireman's pole to get to that front door. When we tried to condense the second "sell" half of the spot, it just took up that much length of time. We couldn't do it. My original conception, by the way — one of the other ideas I chatted about with Ray on trains going home — was to leave everyone up in the attic; but it then seemed like it wasn't doing our good client any "P-T" marketing favor at all by just leaving it there. This couple did take pictures for twenty-five years, but we wanted to show that they were, and still should be, taking pictures, so we felt we had to bring it all down into the present day.

Q. *Ray, you seem to be in charge of a lot of very creative and sensitive people, and you also have to keep your hand on the client's pursestrings. Do you run into much internal conflict in your role?*

MR. FRAGASSO: I think that the success of our Group can be directly attributed to the *rapport* between all the creative forces; copy, art and production. During the nine years I've been in this Group at Thompson, Granger has encouraged this. Everyone is very realistic about their role and their assignment, and we have a very interesting open-door cross-pollenization. It's a very, very free operation. We're constantly exchanging ideas, things we have seen, pieces of music, etc.

MR. DIAMANT: You might enunciate a "Yesterdays" Law: that the quality of the commercial is in direct ratio to the quality of the teamwork.

Q. *Warren suggested that also. Is this typical of the industry, or are you just lucky to have such harmonious working relations?*

MR. THOREN: Well, I second Ray, and I think that goes for Granger, too. It's unbelievable. It's the finest working condition you can find; I'll probably never see it again. I think some of it, too, is due to the nature of the Account. The Account is the best you can work on in this business, above and beyond the client relationship and the product itself. I don't mean to get off into an artsy-fartsy area here, but *when you talk about Kodak commercials, we're making little movies.* Even in the product commercials, it's not an announcer pointing towards the package. It's beautiful little vignettes, and everyone you work with — actors, production house people — becomes a little bit more stimulated, because they know they're

scene 42A

scene 31

scene 42

doing a little *shtick* that's going to be even bigger than getting some nice residual checks. Many things go into it, as Ray says, and it's an unusual group.

MR. FRAGASSO: I like to point one thing out, though. It's an easy misconception to think of the Kodak account as a great account — which it is — but it's not an *easy* account. It's always very difficult to top all the successes we've been enjoying for the past number of years. We do approximately 65 commercials a year, and they all have to sell a lot of product — with style and good advertising. It may look like an easy job because of the way we work at it. We enjoy doing it — but under close examination, it's really a very difficult challenge.

MR. DIAMANT: Ken, Mike Cimino indicated he was rather unhappy with the closing scene: the snapshots and the camera on top of that brown Micarta table. (*scene 42A*) Wasn't that in a sense an announcer "pointing a finger at the product?"

MR. THOREN: That's a hard question, because, as I say, I'd gotten away from the commercial while it was in final production. Just last night, going over the script, I saw I had written that the end product shot should be on the front porch stoop. (*Appendix B, Scene 31*) Why it was never on the stoop, I can't say. I can see Mike's point, even though we are selling good old cameras and film there. But what if the family had put it down? I must ask Warren. You know, if the family had just casually put it down, and Warren took a close shot of it, it would have tied in in a much more related way, than coming out of nowhere onto an ugly desk. I agree with Mike's comments. Where they got off the beam, I don't know.

MR. FRAGASSO: I think I can answer that. (Laughter) You'll notice that after the picture of the Grandparents with the Grandson is taken, we go to a snapshot. (*scene 42*) Kodak doesn't yet have an instant-processing camera, so we needed the opportunity for a juxtaposition of the older snapshots against this new shot of the old couple with the grandchild. I think the transition works very well, because there's a strong, subtle message there about saving all your pictures.

MR. THOREN: Not to wash family laundry, but the shot is not up to the rest of the commercial. (Laughter)

Q. *Granger, do you feel you've had sufficient mileage out of this commercial? As I recall, it's only been aired four times.*

MR. TRIPP: No. I don't think we ever have sufficient mileage out of any of them. We have got the greatest collection of beautiful "motivational" commercials, but as time costs go up, it becomes harder and harder to put them on the air. We didn't get the usage we would like out of any of them. "Sunrise-Sunset" — which won a Grand Prix at Venice — was only used four or five times. "Turn Around" — named a Commercial Classic by the American TV Commercials Festival — was used only two or three times a year when it was current; we would probably still be using it today except that all the pictures were black-and-white, and we haven't found a similar collection in color. No, I don't think any of these spots get on the air as often as I would like to see them. People think Kodak has a lot of money, is a real big-budget spender; but when you break down the Kodak TV advertising budget into all its various categories — supporting film, popular still cameras, fine still cameras, movie cameras, projectors and processing mailers, etc. — there's not that much support money for each. If you look at a schedule of Kodak television commercials, we have about twenty different kinds of Kodak commercials that we make. One reason we make so many each year is that they cover about twenty different subjects. Each of those may be seasonal. "Yesterdays" could run any time, in spite of the fact that the exterior scene is pinned down to an "outdoor" time of year, but many of our commercials are seasonal, so we don't have an unlimited budget to buy time for all the nice commercials we've got. I wish we did.

MR. THOREN: We can take up a collection.

MR. FRAGASSO: I'm here. (Laughter)

MARKET PLANNING

Q. *This is a question for Mr. Shillinglaw, who is also here today. How close was your estimate to the final actual cost of "Yesterdays?"*

MR. SHILLINGLAW: The estimates of the companies we bid were all within about 4%, as I said. That might have meant we were all wrong; as Bill Susman points out, MPO ran into more problems than originally anticipated. That was principally because Mike wanted to put more values into the production. Putting the whole attic on a platform, the overtime shooting — it all added up.

Q. *What was the Client's reactions to those extra prices?*

MR. GENOCK: Oh, there were no "extra prices." This was a bid. That's why I was giving credit to Bill Susman. You see, when you use somebody like Mike Cimino, he may go over and above budget in what is really a search for excellence. I don't think MPO thought it would cost them that much. You heard Warren say how he had wondered what kind of a job Mike might be able to do on "Yesterdays" — although he did a "youth" commercial for us previously, on Flashcubes, and had done some extremely imaginative things. He's just a perfectionist. I'm certainly not sorry for

MPO. I'm sure they got a lot of publicity out of this (Laughter). It's probably the greatest thing they've ever done for themselves.

Q. *Don't you ever pay extra?*

MR. GENOCK: When you have a bid, you pay within it. Unless, of course, you have things like "weather days." There *are* other contingencies, but this was a *firm* production bid.

MR. DIAMANT: MPO still showed a profit that year (Laughter). A fair one, I think.

MR. GENOCK: Not as much as they would have liked. (Laughter)

Q. *Did you get any "feel" on this particular bit of advertising from your own trade — Kodak film and camera marketers?*

MR. GENOCK: No; I wish I did. Kodak is such a large advertiser, I wish I knew a way in which you could separate the different things we do. It's almost impossible. To keep this in perspective, remember the amount of weight put behind this commercial — a two-minute commercial, made originally for the Disney show and also possibly for the Academy Awards. *In today's world, television is becoming so expensive, we're all being driven down to the 30-second, and possibly, before we're through to the 15-second length.* The great challenge now is to make a *very creative* 30-second commercial. The tendency has been to go, somewhat automatically, from a one-minute to a :30. There's a real need now to re-think this whole pattern, because financially, it's the way we're being driven. Especially in the area of expressing mood and emotion, it's becoming more difficult for creative people. After all, television is great for two things: One is demonstration; the other is mood and emotion. And for mood and emotion, you can't suddenly come out of a gripping movie and in thirty seconds set up a completely different situation.

MR. DIAMANT: If it's not impossible, it's extremely difficult to tell the kind of story that "Yesterdays" tells, in thirty seconds. As two-minute and one-minute commercials are pushed aside by :30's, the "story-telling" form is also being pushed aside.

Q. *As commercials become shorter, we're exposed to more and more different kinds of messages within programs. You spoke eloquently about professonalism and the search for excellence. In this welter of fragmented impressions, won't it be extremely difficult for any excellence to stand out?*

MR. GENOCK: Yes. But I think it will also be the greater challenge.

Q. *Isn't there some kind of a Gresham's Law that operates in television commercials — that bad spots tend to drive out good? If we went home tonight and watched television for three hours, we'd see dozens and dozens of commercial messages, until they seemed to be just flying by, kaleidescopically. It's increasingly difficult for viewers to remember the generic products they've just seen, much less the individual advertisers! There doesn't seem to be much impression, or emotional impact.*

MR. GENOCK: I think that's really one of the reasons "specials" have come back into our formats. They allow you to stand out a little with a different length of commercial, and give you a certain stature. The impact is evident. When you consider, for example, how Hallmark comes out on TV only just before their card seasons, yet you don't forget Hallmark. And they exist entirely on "specials." That's my "I" in the formula — you try to get your *Impact* high enough. Just *reach* and *frequency* by themselves over and over again is fine for awareness and slogans, but it doesn't always do the entire job.

MR. DIAMANT: Do you really agree "bad commercials drive out good?" My experience suggests it's been just the other way around. *The creative level, the visual level, the word communication of commercials over the past ten or fifteen years — certainly over the past five years — seems to have been improving.* Of course, that in no way solves "clutter"; it's true that when you break up four one-minute time slots into eight thirty-second time slots, you're doubling the clutter. That may kill commercial television in the end. But it doesn't necessarily mean the messages themselves are getting worse. I like to think they're actually getting a little better. Also, another thing has happened in the last two or three years. The film form, the "look" of television commercials has changed. New techniques and new attitudes are getting messages across much faster than we ever thought possible. The montages, soft-focus, flashes of sunlight, hand-held photography — are all making it possible to register ideas faster than ever before. Despite the fact that time costs keep going up and up, I think that we all may still have a chance to get across some message. It's an interesting thing. The medium *is* really changing. Perhaps we should no longer use a minute to tell many things we told in the past. The world is moving so fast that sixty seconds may be almost too long for many things you see.

MR. HICKS: I think the viewer is already solving a good part of this problem for himself by selectively viewing his commercials. Without even getting up and leaving the room, I think he tunes in and tunes out on commercials, as he sits there. There's no question that the point raised is correct; the increasing *number* of commercials cannot help but produce a negative general effect on the viewer. But like everything else, he then begins to make his own selections. He tends to *really* view fewer of the total number he sees.

MR. DIAMANT: If by some stroke of a Federal pen — if you will — ninety per cent of the commercial time in American television was knocked off the air, and just ten per cent left, I think people would actively look forward to seeing commercials. In the struggle against clutter and all the other competitive problems that beset their clients, I think agencies are now truly on the *qui vive*. They are putting material on the tube that literally transfixes the viewer; it's calculated not to let his attention wander for a second! That's exciting. I have difficulty characterizing it as "bad." If anything, today's poorer commercials are analogous to a sports announcer who says during a ball game, "It's a ball," when you can see it's a ball, and, "It's a strike," when you can clearly see it's a strike. They reiterate what you may already accept as performed fact. Bad commercials are like unimproved radio commercials; they put *words* against an *image* — reiterating the image, holding a mirror against the action. The good commercials are more "posterized"; they know that words are pictures and pictures are words, and you don't necessarily need both together. Frequently an image is stronger; or a word may be stronger. That sophistication makes commercials more penetrating, more indelible. Conceivably in many instances thirty seconds — or even twenty seconds — is sufficient to penetrate an idea. More message would be redundant. Most of the outdoor billboards we remember best we have only seen for three or four seconds — and then out of the corner of our eye. But the impression was strong enough. A few (only a few) words of copy. A very dramatic, image-building picture. And the message is there, and very difficult to escape. And by calling "Yesterdays" "universal," Wally Ross came close to making a point that no one during these last two months has mentioned: that "Yesterdays" — like many other Kodak commercials in this genre — is actually an *old-fashioned silent movie*. An art form, incidentally, in which America gave cards and spades to the rest of the world. American commercials today, with all their flashing images and superimpositions and impressionistic communication are far superior to the way TV commercials first started out, picture against word, word against picture. Now we've moved way beyond that; it's really a leap forward. And it's come only within the last two or three years.

MR. GENOCK: The challenge you're suggesting is that the commercial visual has to be even better than any way that you can *imagine* it. A long time ago, when Eastman Kodak first had the problem of deciding what "flesh color" was, Dr. Mazer — who was head of Research — said, "You'll know when you've got that color. When you feel you want to *pinch* it." (Laughter)

Q. *Are you now at liberty to tell us how much this commercial cost?*

MR. SHILLINGLAW: There's no reason to talk about the cost, simply because it couldn't be duplicated today at that price.

MR. DIAMANT: Sel, can we approach it a bit differently? Suppose Ken, or Warren or Granger suggested a one-minute commercial today, somewhat similar to "Yesterdays," can we have a rough idea of what it might cost?

MR. SHILLINGLAW: I'm a bad guesser. (Laughter) See me after the meeting.

Appendix B

Copywriter Ken Thoren's original draft script for a two-minute TV color film commercial for Eastman Kodak, to run a year later in the Disney show "Wonderful World of Color." (April 15, 1966.)

EASTMAN KODAK TV COMMERCIAL   April 15, 1966
DISNEY: 1967
P-T STILLS: "YESTERDAYS"
TWO-MINUTE COLOR FILM

(N.B.: PEG AND HARRY MANN HAVE BEEN MARRIED FOR TWENTY-EIGHT
YEARS OR AT LEAST THEY WILL HAVE BEEN, COME NEXT MONTH.
THEIR TWO SONS, HOLT AND CLAY, HAVE MARRIED AND HAVE STARTED
FAMILIES OF THEIR OWN.

THIS DAY PEG HAS FINALLY FINAGLED HARRY INTO HELPING HER
CLEAN UP THE CELLAR. WHILE SORTING OUT THINGS, PEG DISCOVERS
A LARGE WOBBLY CARDBOARD CARTON, STUFFED WITH SNAPSHOTS. SHE
AND HARRY START TO PEEL THROUGH THEM, THEIR JOB TOTALLY
FORGOTTEN.)

PRODUCTION NOTE: THE OPTIMUM WOULD BE TO FIND A MARRIED ACTOR
COUPLE ABOUT THE SAME AGE AS THE SCRIPT RECOMMENDS. IN CASTING,
ONE PREREQUISITE WOULD BE TO HAVE THE ACTORS COME TO THE
SESSIONS WITH A COLLECTION OF THEIR OWN SNAPSHOTS, COVERING
TWENTY YEARS OR SO OF THEIR LIVES TOGETHER. IF THIS PROVES
FUTILE, IT SHOULDN'T PROVE TOO DIFFICULT TO FIND AN ACTUAL
COUPLE--NON-PROFESSIONALS, THAT IS--WHO ANSWER OUR REQUIRE-
MENTS.

VIDEO	AUDIO
1. FADE UP ON DOLLY SHOT MOVING TOWARDS OPEN CELLAR WINDOW FROM THE OUTSIDE. SUPER: "KODAK".	(SFX: OUTDOORS SOUNDS: I.E., BIRDS, KIDS PLAYING DOWN THE STREET, LAWN MOWER.)
2. CROSS DISSOLVE TO INTERIOR OF CELLAR AND CONTINUE TO DOLLY. WE SEE A CLUTTERED AND YET NOT DISREPUTABLE LOOKING COLLECTION OF PROPS ANY FAMILY MIGHT COLLECT OVER THE YEARS: TOYS, A CRIB FILLED WITH BOXES, CHRISTMAS DECORATIONS, A FEW PIECES OF OLD FURNITURE, ETC.	(WE HEAR PEG AND HARRY TALKING TO EACH OTHER BUT THEIR VOICES ARE SO LOW, IT'S ALMOST AS IF WE WERE EAVESDROPPING. THEIR REMARKS ARE AD LIB.)
3. DISSOLVE TO MEDIUM SHOT OF HARRY STANDING NEXT TO AN OLD WIND-UP VICTROLA WITH ITS LID UP. HE'S OPENED FRONT DOORS AND HAS TAKEN OUT A STACK OF RECORDS.	

VIDEO	AUDIO

VIDEO

4. DISSOLVE TO CLOSE SHOT OF PEG AS SHE PICKS UP A TATTERED OLD TEDDY BEAR. SHE LOOKS AT IT, REMEMBERING THE DAYS HOLT -- OR WAS IT CLAY?--CARRIED IT EVERYWHERE.

5. DISSOLVE TO LONG SHOT AS PEG PUTS TOY IN BOX AND THEN TURNS TO LIFT LARGE CARDBOARD CARTON.

6. CUT TO SHOT OF HARRY LOOKING REFLECTIVELY AT A RECORD. HE WINDS UP VICTROLA AND STARTS TO PUT RECORD ON TURNTABLE.

7. CUT TO PEG AS SHE ALMOST DROPS HEAVY CARTON. LID COMES OFF.

8. CUT TO TIGHT SHOT OF CARTON. LIKE MOST PEOPLE, THE MANNS NEVER WERE "ALBUM-KEEPERS". FOR YEARS, THEY MERELY STUFFED ALL THEIR SNAPSHOTS INTO THE TOP DRAWER OF THE DINING ROOM CHEST. WHEN THAT BEGAN TO OVERFLOW, THEY PUT ALL THEIR PICTURES INTO THIS CARTON. WE SEE IT'S HAPHAZARDLY STUFFED WITH NOT ONLY PICTURES BUT ALSO OLD NEWSPAPERS, PROGRAMS, MENUS, ETC.

9. CUT TO WIDER SHOT OF PEG AS SHE PUTS CARTON ON FLOOR. SHE SITS IN MOTHY OVERSTUFFED CHAIR AND ASKS HARRY TO JOIN HER.

10. CUT TO TIGHT SHOT OF HARRY PUTTING NEEDLE ON RECORD.

11. PULL BACK AS HE GOES TO JOIN PEG.

AUDIO

(MUSIC: THE RECORD STARTS. THE SONG IS "YESTERDAYS". WE EITHER SIMULATE THE ARRANGEMENT AND THE SOUND OF A 30'S SINGER, OR WE SEARCH FOR AN ACTUAL RECORDING OF THE SONG OF THAT TIME.)

VIDEO	AUDIO
12. CUT TO MEDIUM SHOT OF PEG AND HARRY LOOKING AT SNAPSHOTS.	SINGER: Yesterdays, yesterdays . . .
13. CUT TO SNAPSHOT: PEG AND HARRY IN THEIR EARLY TWENTIES IN BRAND-NEW CAR. PEG SITS IN RUMBLE SEAT, SMILING AT CAMERA.	Days I knew as happy . . .
14. CUT TO SNAPSHOT: PEG AND HARRY ON A PICNIC. (NATURALLY, THESE ARE ONLY SUGGESTED SHOTS. THE REAL THING OR ACTUAL PICTURES WOULD BE USED.)	. . . sweet sequester'd days.
15. CUT TO TWO-SHOT OF HARRY AND PEG ENJOYING THEIR PICTURES.	Olden days,
16. CUT TO SNAPSHOT: WEDDING POSE.	Golden days,
17. CUT TO SNAPSHOT: HONEYMOON SHOT.	Days of mad romance . . .
18. CUT TO SNAPSHOT: CU OF PEG.	. . . and love.
19. CUT TO SNAPSHOT: PEG AND HARRY WITH HOLT, THEIR FIRST BORN.	Then gay youth was mine,
20. CUT TO SNAPSHOT: PEG WITH TWO-YEAR-OLD HOLT AND CLAY, AN INFANT IN HER ARMS.	Truth was mine.
21. CUT TO SNAPSHOT: FAMILY ALL TOGETHER. BOYS A LITTLE OLDER AND HARRY IN ARMY UNIFORM.	Joyous, free . . .
22. CUT TO SNAPSHOT: BOYS WITH HARRY. THEY'RE STILL A LITTLE OLDER. HE'S BACK IN CIVVIES AGAIN.	. . . and flaming life . . .
23. CUT TO SNAPSHOT: HARRY AND PEG STAND WITH HOLT IN HIS COLLEGE CAP AND GOWN.	. . . forsooth, was mine.

VIDEO	AUDIO
24. CUT TO TIGHT SHOT OF PEG STILL LOOKING AT PICTURES. HER FACE REFLECTS A POIGNANT FEELING BUT THEN	Sad am I . . .
25. BREAKS INTO AN OPEN LAUGH AS CAMERA PULLS BACK TO INCLUDE HARRY WHO'S SHOWING PEG A SHOT HE HAS FOUND.	Glad am I . . .
26. HOLD AS PEG AND HARRY EXCHANGE LOVING LOOKS.	For today I'm dreaming of yesterdays.
27. THEIR SPELL IS BROKEN AT SOUND OF CAR HORN. BOTH LOOK OFF SCREEN AND QUICKLY GET UP AND LEAVE.	(SFX: CAR HORN BLOWS OUTSIDE.) (MUSIC: SEGUE TO MODERN, UNDERSCORING ARRANGEMENT OF "YESTERDAYS".)
28. DISSOLVE TO FRONT PORCH AS HARRY AND PEG HURRY OUT TO GREET HOLT, HIS WIFE AND THEIR LITTLE GIRL WHO HAVE JUST DRIVEN OVER FOR A VISIT.	(SFX: AS BEFORE, WE HEAR AD LIB REMARKS UNDER THE MUSIC -- AS IF WE WERE BYSTANDERS AT SCENE.)
29. DISSOLVE TO SHOT OF HARRY TAKING A PICTURE OF GRANDDAUGHTER WITH KODAK INSTAMATIC 104.	
30. DISSOLVE TO A MONTAGE OF STILLS: SHOWING HARRY, PEG, HOLT, DAUGHTER-IN-LAW AND GRANDDAUGHTER IN VARIOUS POSES.	ANNOUNCER: (V.O.) Yesterdays . . . today . . . and tomorrow . . . are yours to keep -- in pictures.
31. CUT TO SHOT OF CAMERA AND FILM SITTING ON FRONT STOOP.	All it takes is a camera, Kodak film and a little thoughtfulness. (MUSIC: UP AND OUT.)

STORYBOARD GLOSSARY

Standard abbreviations and terms used to describe picture framing (composition), camera movement and voice sources.

*   *   *

VIDEO:

FS = Full Shot = The actors and the entire background scene are in frame.
MS = Medium Shot = The actors' whole bodies are in frame.
MCU = Medium close-up = The actors are waist-up.
CU = Close-up = The actors' faces.
ECU = Extra Close-up = The actors' features.

*   *   *

DOLLY (In or Out) = Slow frame change accomplished by moving the camera forward or backward (altering parallax).
TRUCK = Slow frame change accomplished by moving the camera sideways.
PAN (Left or Right) = Camera movement from a set position, along a horizontal arc.
TILT = (Up or Down) = Camera movement from a set position, along a vertical arc.

*   *   *

AUDIO:

O.C. = On Camera = Someone visible says something.
V.O. = Voice Over = Someone invisible says something.

*   *   *

The following editing terms describe techniques for montaging from one frame of picture information to another:
DISSOLVE = Fade-in of a new scene over the fade-out of the previous one.
CUT = Instantaneous replacement of a frame with one completely new.
POP = (On or Off) = Instantaneous addition or subtraction of new information (usually artwork or titles).
LOGO = Logotype = The advertiser's individualized graphic design of his name, etc.

Appendix C

"YESTERDAYS"

(as produced)

JWT #68-0130-120

MPO #5450

A two-minute color television film commercial created by J. Walter Thompson Co., and produced by MPO Videotronics, Inc. for the Eastman Kodak Company. Initial broadcast: July 23, 1967.

VIDEO

1. (01½ - 40f - 0:01½)

    OPEN ON "KODAK" LOGO SUPERED
    LOWER RIGHT FRAME OVER EXTERIOR
    CU ATTIC WINDOW. DOLLY IN.

VIDEO

1A. (:02½ - 56f - 0:04)

    LOSE SUPER AS
    FATHER STANDS UP INSIDE WINDOW,
    BLOWING DUST OFF CARDBOARD BOX.
    MOTHER IN BACKGROUND

        AUDIO

        FATHER (O.C.): All right.

        Where do you want this?

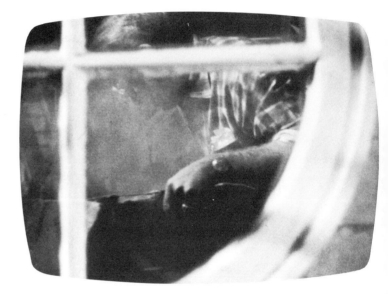

VIDEO

2. (:01 - 21f - 0:05)

    CUT TO LOW INTERIOR TRUCKING FS OF
    CLUTTERED ATTIC. FATHER CARRIES
    BOX PAST MOTHER, DROPS IT. IT
    SPILLS OPEN.

        AUDIO

        (TRIPPING) Hiiiii!   Wha!

164

VIDEO

3. (:01½ - 31f - 0:06)

CUT TO LOW MCU AS MOTHER LOOKS
UP, AMUSED.

AUDIO

MOTHER (O.C.): (LAUGHS)

VIDEO

4. (:03½ - 80f - 0:09½)

CUT TO LOW MS OF MOTHER WIPING
DUST OFF CHAIR. SHE WIPES HER
HANDS AND SITS DOWN. FATHER AT
VICTROLA IN BACKGROUND.

VIDEO

5. (:01 - 29f - 0:10½)

CUT TO LOW CU FATHER BLOWING
DUST OFF VICTROLA COVER AND
LIFTING IT.

VIDEO

6. (:02½ - 57f - 0:13)

    CUT TO HIGH MS MOTHER OPENING
    BOX ON HER LAP FILLED WITH OLD
    SNAPSHOTS. OLD RECORDS ON FLOOR.

VIDEO

7. (:03½ - 86f - 0:16½)

    CUT TO LOW MS MOTHER
    EXAMINING SNAPSHOTS AS
    FATHER BLOWS DUST OFF OLD
    RECORD AND PUTS IT ON
    VICTROLA.

VIDEO

8. (:02½ - 58f - 0:19)

    CUT TO CU FATHER'S HAND
    PUTTING NEEDLE ON RECORD.

    AUDIO

    (MUSIC: SCRATCHY ACOUSTIC
    RECORDING OF "YESTERDAYS".)

VIDEO

(:06 - 147f - 0:25)

CUT TO LOW MCU FATHER
PAN AND TILT WITH HIM AS
HE PICKS UP OLD FOOTBALL
AND SITS NEXT TO MOTHER,
SHE SHOWS HIM OLD SNAPSHOT.

AUDIO

FEMALE VOCALIST (V.O.):

Yesterdays...

VIDEO

(:04 - 92f - 0:29)

CUT TO HIGH CU OF HANDS
HOLDING B/W SNAPSHOT: FS
YOUNGER FATHER AND MOTHER
IN 1930's ROADSTER

AUDIO

Yesterdays...

FATHER (V.O.. UNDER):
(LAUGHS) How do you like
those pants, anyway?

VIDEO

A. (:02½ - 58f - 0:31)

HANDS BRING IN ANOTHER B/W
SNAPSHOT: CU YOUNGER FATHER
AND MOTHER. LIVE FINGER POINTS
OUT HER HAIRDO.

AUDIO

VOCALIST (V.O.): Days I
knew as happy...

MOTHER (V.O.. UNDER): This
was smart of me.

VIDEO

11. (:02½ - 60f - 0:33½)

CUT TO LOW REVERSE ECU FATHER,
RUBBING HEAD IN DISBELIEF.

AUDIO

VOCALIST (V.O.): ...sweet

sequester'd...

VIDEO

12. (:02½ - 66f - 0:36)

CUT TO HIGH ECU HANDS TURNING
OVER ANOTHER B/W SNAPSHOT:
MS YOUNGER FATHER AND MOTHER ON
COLLEGE STEPS.

AUDIO

...days.
FATHER (V.O.. UNDER): My
mistake was starting
carrying your books.

VIDEO

13. (:03 - 67f - 0:39)

CUT TO LOW REVERSE ECU FATHER AND
MOTHER SMILING AT EACH OTHER.

AUDIO

VOCALIST (V.O.): Olden Days...

VIDEO

14. (:02½ - 55f - 0:41½)

CUT TO HIGH CU HAND TURNING
OVER B/W SNAPSHOT: MS WEDDING
PHOTO IN OVAL FRAME.

AUDIO

Golden...

VIDEO

15. (:01 - 28f - 0:42½)

CUT TO LOW REVERSE ECU FATHER
STUDYING OVAL PHOTO.

AUDIO

...days.

VIDEO

16. (:01 - 28f - 0:43½)

CUT TO HIGH ECU HAND TAKING
WEDDING PHOTO OUT OF FRAME.

169

VIDEO

17. (:03 - 73f - 0:46½)

CUT TO HIGH ECU MOTHER'S HAND
BRINGING IN ANOTHER B/W
SNAPSHOT: FS YOUNGER MOTHER
AND FATHER WITH SKIS IN SNOW.

AUDIO

Days of Mad Romance...

VIDEO

18. (:02½ - 66f - 0:49)

CUT TO LOW ECU FATHER
STUDYING SNAPSHOT. MOTHER
SMOOTHS HAIR IN FOREGROUND.

AUDIO

...and love.

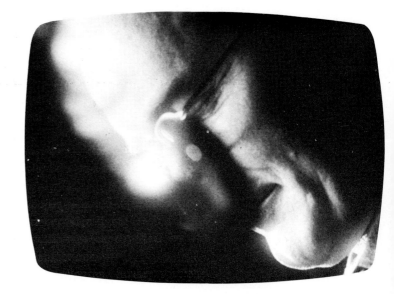

VIDEO

19. (:02½ - 62f - 0:51½)

CUT TO HIGH ECU B/W SNAPSHOT:
MS YOUNGER MOTHER WITH HER
TWO YOUNG BOYS OUTSIDE
BARBER SHOP. MOTHER'S HANDS
MOVE SNAPSHOT OUT OF FRAME.

AUDIO

(MUSIC: LOSES SCRATCHY
SURFACE NOISE, CHANGES TO CONTEMPORARY
ELECTRONIC EQUALIZATION.)

170

Then gay youth was mine.

VIDEO

20. (:03½ - 80f - 0:55)

CUT TO HIGH CU AS FATHER'S
HANDS BRING IN ANOTHER B/W
SNAPSHOT: MOTHER, WITH
FATHER IN WORLD WAR II
UNIFORM. FATHER'S HAND
REMOVES EYEGLASSES IN
FOREGROUND.

AUDIO

Truth...

VIDEO

21. (:01½ - 30f - 0:56½)

CUT TO LOW REVERSE ECU AS
FATHER REMOVES EYEGLASSES TO
STUDY SNAPSHOT.

AUDIO

...was mine.

VIDEO

22. (:03½ - 80f - 1:00)

CUT TO HIGH ECU COLOR SNAPSHOT:
MCU MOTHER, WITH SON IN
FOOTBALL UNIFORM. FATHER'S
FINGER POINTS TO FOOTBALL.

AUDIO

Joyous, free and flaming...

171

VIDEO

23. (:01 - 24f - 1:01)

CUT TO LOW REVERSE MS FATHER
AND MOTHER STUDYING SNAPSHOT.
FATHER STARTS TO PUT EYEGLASSES
BACK ON.

AUDIO

...life...

VIDEO

24. (:03 - 70f - 1:03½)

CUT TO HIGH CU FATHER'S EYEGLASSES
PASSING IN FRONT OF ANOTHER COLOR
SNAPSHOT: FS FAMILY AT GRADUATION.

AUDIO

...forsooth, was mine.

VIDEO

25. (:02½ - 60f - 1:06)

CUT TO LOW REVERSE ECU FATHER
STUDYING SNAPSHOT.

AUDIO

Sad am I.

VIDEO

26. (:03 - 68f - 1:09)

CUT TO LOW ECU MOTHER LAUGHING
AT ANOTHER SNAPSHOT.

AUDIO

Glad am...

VIDEO

27. (:02 - 48f - 1:11)

CUT TO HIGH CU HANDS SHUFFLING
ADDITIONAL SNAPSHOTS.

AUDIO

...I.

VIDEO

28. (:02 - 45f - 1:13)

CUT TO LOW REVERSE ECU MOTHER AND
FATHER STUDYING SNAPSHOTS.

AUDIO

For today...

173

VIDEO

29. (:03 - 75f - 1:16)

CUT TO HIGH ECU B/W SNAPSHOT:
FS SON, SON'S WIFE, BABY
GRANDSON.

AUDIO

...I'm dreaming of...
(SOUND: AUTO HORN
BLOWING, OFF.)

VIDEO

30. (:04 - 90f - 1:20)

CUT TO MCU FATHER AND MOTHER,
HEADS IN SILHOUETTE.

AUDIO

(MUSIC: RETURNS TO
SCRATCHY, ACOUSTIC
CHARACTER.)

...yester...

MOTHER (O.C., UNDER): It's
almost four o'clock!
VOCALIST (V.O.): ...yester...yester...yester...

VIDEO

31. (:03½ - 83f - 1:23½)

CUT TO CU VICTROLA TURNTABLE.
DOLLY BACK AS FATHER'S HAND ENTERS
FRAME TO LIFT NEEDLE OFF BROKEN
RECORD.

AUDIO

VOCALIST (V.O.): (STOPS)

VIDEO

32. (:01½ - 37f - 1:24½)

CUT TO LOW FS CLUTTERED ATTIC AS
MOTHER STARTS DOWN STAIRS.

VIDEO

33. (:02 - 48f - 1:26½)

CUT TO INTERIOR MS FATHER
WITH FOOTBALL RUNNING TOWARD
ATTIC WINDOW. CAMERA TRUCKS
THROUGH IMAGINARY WALL TO FRAME
EXTERIOR MS FATHER LEANING OUT
WINDOW.

VIDEO

34. (:03 - 76f - 1:29½)

CUT TO EXTERIOR MS MOTHER RUNNING DOW
PORCH STEPS. PAN RIGHT AS SHE GRABS
GRANDSON WHILE SON AND WIFE RUN IN
FROM RIGHT FRAME TO KISS HER.

AUDIO

(MUSIC: CONTEMPORARY
ORCHESTRATION OF
"YESTERDAYS".)

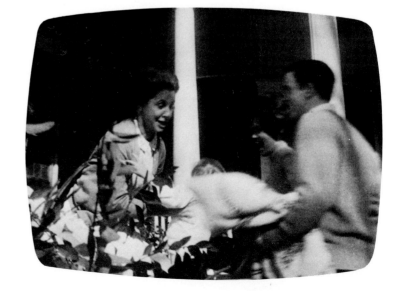

VIDEO

34A. (:01½ - 36f - 1:31)

TILT UP TO FS FATHER WITH
FOOTBALL IN ATTIC WINDOW. HE
TOSSES BALL DOWN TO SON.

VIDEO

35. (:01 - 20f - 1:32)

CUT TO MCU 3-SHOT: EXCITED MOTHER,
HOLDING GRANDSON, WIFE.

VIDEO

36. (:01 - 25f - 1:33)

CUT TO REVERSE CU 3-SHOT: EXCITED
SON, GRANDSON, WIFE.

VIDEO

37. (:03 - 77f - 1:36)

CUT TO MS 5-SHOT: MOTHER, SON,
GRANDSON, WIFE, AS FATHER RUNS
OUT ONTO PORCH. PAN AS HE CATCHES
FOOTBALL THROW FROM SON, HUGS HIM,
KISSES WIFE.

VIDEO

38. (:01½ - 38f - 1:38)

CUT TO MCU 5-SHOT AS WIFE
WITH CAMERA LEAVES GROUP.

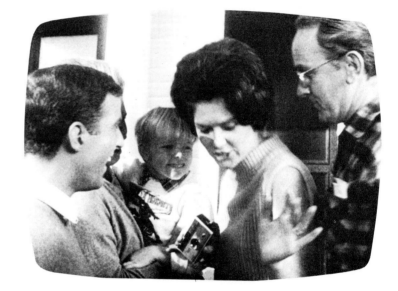

VIDEO

39. (:01 - 25f - 1:39)

CUT TO REVERSE ECU WIFE
AIMING 104 KODAK INSTAMATIC.

VIDEO

40. (:02 - 54f - 1:41)

CUT TO HIGH (SIDE) MCU
3-SHOT: FATHER, MOTHER
HOLDING GRANDSON, POSING
FOR WIFE'S INSTAMATIC.

VIDEO

41. (:01½ - 41f - 1:42½)

CUT TO REVERSE FS WIFE
WITH CAMERA. SON BEHIND HER.

VIDEO

42. (:06½ - 154f - 1:49)

CUT TO ECU COLOR SNAPSHOT: SAME
MS 3-SHOT MOTHER HOLDING GRANDSON,
FATHER, DOLLY BACK TO MCU TO
REVEAL MOTHER'S HAND IS HOLDING
SNAPSHOT WITH OLDER B/W SNAPSHOT
(SCENE 29). OTHER OLD SNAPSHOTS
REPRISED ON TABLE IN BACKGROUND.

AUDIO

ANNOUNCER (V.O.): Yesterday...
today... and tomorrow... are
yours to keep in pictures.
All it takes is a camera--

178

VIDEO

42A. (:06½ - 153f - 1:55½)

PAN SLOWLY RIGHT TO FRAME MCU
KODAK FILM PACKAGE WITH 104
INSTAMATIC CAMERA.

AUDIO

--Kodak film... and a
little thoughtfulness.
VOCALIST (V.O.): Yesterdays.

VIDEO

42B. (:04½ - 107f - 2:00)

POP ON "KODAK" LOGO IN UPPER RIGHT FRAME.

179

Appendix D

WORKSHOP PARTICIPANTS

CLIENT: E. P. Genock

AGENCY:
Warren P. Aldoretta
Alan H. Anderson
Raymond Fragasso
Matthew Harlib
Wyatte Hicks
Harry L. Leighton
Evelyn Barnes Pierce
Justine M. Somers
Stanley Tarner
Harold M. Taylor
Alfred R. Tennyson
Kenneth A. Thoren
Granger Tripp
Selwyn Shillinglaw
Joyce Hsu
Marion Preston

PRODUCTION HOUSE:
Michael Cimino
George Fineman
Karl Hueglin
Gerald Hirschfeld
William Susman

CREATIVE SUPPLIERS:
Charles Ahto
Michael "Kipp" Currie
James Fagas
(Otto Harbach)
(Jerome Kern)
Sarah Meade
Robert D. Pittluck
Sol Tabachnick
Wallace A. Ross

CHAIRMAN: Lincoln Diamant

General Glossary

acoustic recording — early non-electronic recording technique.

affiliate — TV station carrying programs of one of the three major networks.

AFM — American Federation of Musicians; the musicians' union.

AFTRA — American Federation of Radio and Television Artists; performers' union covering radio and video tape talent.

American Television Commercials Festival — an annual TV awards presentation.

answer print — first print made from the completed optical negative and track for approval.

Arriflex — German motion picture camera originally used in the Wehrmacht.

art director — advertising agency specialist charged with visual responsibilities.

ASCAP — American Society of Composers, Authors & Publishers; trade guild of compositional talent. See: *credits*.

audio — relating to the sound portion of a TV commercial. See: *mix*.

audio tape — magnetic oxide-coated tape used in electronic sound recording.

blocking — roughing out camera and cast positions and movement in advance of filming.

BMI — Broadcast Music, Inc.; trade guild of compositional talent. See: *credits*.

can — container for film elements.

check print — quick "slop" print from the completed optical picture negative (only) to check mechanical printing errors.

China Girl — identical piece of negative of an American girl used in all U.S. film laboratories as a color printing standard.

cineboard — 16mm motion picture version of a storyboard, photographed from the storyboard frames themselves.

cinema verité — documentary style imposed on non-documentary filming.

Cinex — strip of film of a particular scene. Each frame is printed in a slightly different color balance, for selection purposes.

closed-circuit — non-broadcast transmission of a television image to a receiver.

color balance — **proper** selection of magenta, **cyan** and yellow elements to **give the most** effective picture.

composite — talent photographic sheet with credits.

composite print — film print containing both picture and sound track.

cone — huge reflector for lighting large set areas.

contact print — 16mm print made from a 16mm negative.

corporate campaign — advertising campaign charged with developing a corporate "image", as apart from selling a particular product.

costume house — rental agency for talent wardrobe.

CPM — cost per thousand; evaluation of the cost of an advertising campaign in terms of the audience reached.

credits — elaborate point system established by ASCAP to distribute royalties on the basis of frequency of composition performance.

cue — signal to begin presentation of a new element.

cue sheet — written collection of sequential cues.

cut — editing to a new element directly from an old one.

cyan — greenish-blue element of a color print.

dailies — one-light positive prints from negative material filmed the previous day.

delayed broadcast — programs — usually on 16mm film — broadcast over stations with no direct network cable or microwave link; *DB's.*

demographics — breakdown of a broadcast audience by varying characteristics.

dissolve — fading into a new scene while fading out an old one.

dolly — wheeled motion picture camera mount. Also; the visual effect of a camera move on such a mount.

dub — copy of a magnetic recording.

dubber — playback equipment for magnetically recorded sprocketed film.

echo chamber — device for adding artificial echo to an electronic recording signal.

edge number — multi-digit consecutive number identifying each foot of raw film stock, applied by the manufacturer.

editor — production house specialist charged with piecing together a film commercial from different visual and sound elements.

8mm — film stock 8mm wide.

electronic recording — conversion of sound waves into recorded electrical impulses.

exterior — the outside of a set or location.

fade-in, -out — transition from a black screen to an image; vice-versa.

filter (audio) — deliberate constriction of recorded frequencies to achieve a tinny or bassy effect.

filter (video) — deliberate alteration of a film image by shaded or tinted glass over the camera lens.

fine cut — final, approved work print.

finegrain — special raw stock with a more transparent base and more sensitive emulsion characteristics.

footage — film measurement reference; each foot of 35mm film contains sixteen frames; each foot of 16mm film contains 40 frames.

foot candle — a luminance standard for projection.

f.p.s. — frames per second.

frame — the individual picture element in any size motion picture film; 24 frames are exposed each second by cameras running at normal sound speed.

freeze — repetition of the identical motion picture frame, usually giving the effect of a somewhat blurred still picture.

frequency — the number of times an advertising message is exposed to the identical audience.

full coat — magnetic oxide-coated 35mm film used for multitrack recording.

fuller's earth — a claylike material that absorbs oils and grease.

gate — projector opening through which light passes through the film onto the screen.

generation — duplicate copy of a master, usually made with some loss of quality.

grips — film crew members charged with lifting and carrying.

guide track — temporary sound track prepared only as a general guide to subsequent photography.

integration — physical editing of a film commercial into a TV film program.

interior — the inside of a set or location.

interlock — mechanical linkage of separate picture and sound-on-film elements, held in synchronization by sprocket holes.

internegative — finegrain optical color negative made from interpositive materials.

interpositive — finegrain color positive made from a selected piece of original camera negative. Used to make an internegative.

level — sound recording volume.

lighting grid — metal framework for suspending lights over a set.

location — non-studio area for photography.

log — written record.

magenta — purplish-red element of a color print.

magnetic recording — sound recording effected by changing the polarity of microscopic particles of iron oxide on film or tape.

mag stripe — clear 35mm sprocketed film with a strip of magnetic oxide for recording a single track.

major sponsor — the advertiser with the most commercials on a multiple-sponsored program.

marketing — all aspects of product distribution and sales.

master — an original final version.

M & E — music and effects soundtracks.

medium — means of communicating an advertising message.

Mitchell — American-made motion picture camera.

mix — re-recording of several audio elements into a single soundtrack.

monitor — any TV receiver connected to a transmission source by wire.

Moviola — complicated sound-and-film editing machine.

multiple image — frame composed of several different picture sources.

needle drop — stock music term covering usage of licensed musical material.

network — one of three huge combines supplying program and advertising material to U.S. television stations.

on camera — talent performing in front of a camera. See: *voice-over.*

one-light print — positive film material printed with no individual color corrections.

optical house — facility for processing the final picture negative and including all editing and titling effects.

optical negative — final printing negative (picture).

optical track — final printing negative (sound)

opticals — colloquial term for wipes, dissolves, superimpositions and similar effects.

origination point — network feed points, usually New York or Los Angeles.

pan — camera movement in a horizontal direction. See: *tilt.*

P.D. — public domain; the status of a creative work whose copyright has expired.

pedestal — electronic calibration of certain TV picture characteristics.

Polaroid — an instant-processing camera; its film.

position — location of a commercial within a program format.

print — 1. a positive copy of a film negative. 2. space advertising in newspapers and magazines.

printer — optical machine for exposing a film negative/print.

producer — advertising agency specialist charged with production responsibilities.

props — film crew members charged with handling photographic properties.

raw stock — unexposed motion picture film.

reach — the number of times the same advertising message is exposed to different audiences.

reduction print — 16mm print made optically from a 35mm negative.

reel, sample — best examples of a film craftsman's work.

reflectors — tiltable shiny surfaces for reflecting sunlight on location.

release print — final print for TV broadcast.

renderer — agency artist who realistically renders an art director's doodles.

residual — re-payment for continued commercial use under talent union codes.

rights — creative equity.

rough cut — first attempt at editing the commercial picture.

SAG — Screen Actors' Guild; the performers' union covering film talent.

scatter plan — a carefully random advertising schedule.

scratch track — See: *guide track.*

SEG — Screen Extras' Guild; the extras' union for film.

segué — fading one audio element into another.

78rpm — standard rpm disc recording speed prior to LP recording.

shtick — a small part of a larger performance.

16mm — film stock 16mm wide.

snorkel — long, thin camera lens attachment.

sonic cleaner — film cleaning apparatus utilizing sound waves.

soundtrack — 1. *optical:* recorded light patterns that can be translated back into sound waves. 2. *magnetic:* recorded magnetic patterns that can be translated back into sound waves.

sound reader — editing machine for achieving either of the above translations.

special — a specially-scheduled one-time TV program.

splicer — cutting device for exactly adhering two different pieces of film.

spot — colloquial term for *commercial.*

sprocketed film — standard film with sprocket holes.

start mark — physical mark at the head of a piece of film, used for synchronization.

still — a single photograph.

stock music — previously-recorded "library" music for licensed use.

storyboard — two-dimensional visualization, usually on paper in separated frames, of a television commercial.

Super 8 — A new form of 8mm film.

sync, synchronization — exact matching of sound and picture elements.

synchronizer — editing machine for accomplishing the above.

system — See: *closed-circuit.*

35mm — film stock 35mm wide.

Tijuana — style of orchestration utilizing massed horns.

tilt — camera movement in a vertical direction. See: *pan.*

timing — control of light through a negative element during printing.

traffic — control of film requirements for broadcast advertising.

track — See: *soundtrack.*

unit manager — network employee with coordination responsibilities for advertising material in a particular program.

video — relating to the picture portion of a TV commercial.

video analyzer — complicated electronic device for establishing correct color balance for an optical negative.

video tape — magnetic-oxide tape capable of recording a color TV picture and sound.

voice-over — off-camera voice or announcer.

wild spot — television commercial broadcast locally during a station break.

work print — picture sequence assembled by an editor for final approval.

xenon — motion picture lamp containing xenon gas for truer color projection.

Index

22; Fashion Department at, 86-88; Kodak production team at, 80, 85, 88, 111, 143; management supervisor at, 118-20; music and talent negotiator at, 31-35; music producer at, 18, 37-39; producer at, 36, 37, 38, 47-51, 61-62, 78-81; and production group head, 111-12; production supervisor at, 16-20, 35-37; quality control supervisor at, 29; stylist at, 86-88; talent and music negotiator at, 31-35; traffic manager at, 22-24; TV Editorial Group at, 20, 22, 23; and writer, 96-98; *see also* MPO Videotronics, Inc.; "Yesterdays"

Thoren, Kenneth A., 13, 15, 48, 93, 95, 96, 101, 111, 122, 123, 142, 145, 157; in panel discussion, 146, 147, 148, 149, 150, 151

Thrift shops, as source of props, 90

"Tijuana" sound, 36, 37, 38, 40

Timing correction strip, 25

Traffic manager, 22-24

Tripp, Granger, 80, 93, 94, 96, 97, 99, 100, 108, 122, 124, 143; in panel discussion, 145, 146, 147, 148, 150-51

"Turn Around," 124, 148, 151

TV Commercial Production Workshop (International Radio & Television Society), 9, 11, 125 *ff*.

Verichrome Flm, Kodak, 72

"Way You Look Tonight, The," 95, 124, 148

"Wild spot," 32, 34, 147

Wilder, Joe, 40

"Wonderful World of Color, The," 20, 21, 127, 128, 157

Workprint markings, standard, to indicate effects, 60

Writer, 96-98

Xenon, 29

"Yesterdays," 10, 13, 15, 16, 19-23 *passim*, 32-40 *passim*, 59, 61, 62, 64, 74, 75, 78, 79, 93, 95, 113, 116-24 *passim*, 131, 132, 133, 134, 154; actors in, 51, 52, 65, 67, 68, 69, 73, 75-77, 85; answer prints on, 29, 30, 129; attic scene in, 89-90, 91, 92, 98, 111, 138, 140; awards won by, 114, 115, 116, 129; casting sessions for, 65, 85; costs of, 64, 69, 82-83, 151, 155; motivation build-up of, 48; as "picture-taking" commercial, 21; printing stage of 24-28; script for, 96-98, 101, 157-161; 163-169; sound mixing of, 41-46; storyboard of, 78, 99, 100, 101, 102-107, 110, 145, 146; time required for production of, 18, 129, 130; wedding scene in, 68, 69, 87; *see also* MPO Videotronics, Inc.; Thompson Company, J. Walter